MW00800617

SUFFRAGE AND ITS LIMITS

SUFFRAGE AND ITS LIMITS

The New York Story

Edited by

KATHLEEN M. DOWLEY,
SUSAN INGALLS LEWIS,
AND MEG DEVLIN O'SULLIVAN

Top cover image: Suffragists "march in October 1917, displaying placards containing the signatures of over one million New York women demanding to vote." October 1917, the *New York Times* photo archive.

Published by State University of New York Press, Albany

© 2020 State University of New York

All rights reserved

No part of this book may be used or reproduced in any manner whatsoever without written permission. No part of this book may be stored in a retrieval system or transmitted in any form or by any means including electronic, electrostatic, magnetic tape, mechanical, photocopying, recording, or otherwise without the prior permission in writing of the publisher.

For information, contact State University of New York Press, Albany, NY
www.sunypress.edu

Library of Congress Cataloging-in-Publication Data

Names: Dowley, Kathleen M., 1967– editor. | Lewis, Susan Ingalls, 1949–
    editor. | O'Sullivan, Meg Devlin, 1978– editor.
Title: Suffrage and its limits : the New York story / [edited by] Kathleen M.
    Dowley, Susan Ingalls Lewis, Meg Devlin O'Sullivan.
Description: Albany : State University of New York Press, [2020] | Includes
    bibliographical references and index.
Identifiers: LCCN 2019032772 | ISBN 9781438479699 (hardcover : alk.
    paper) | ISBN 9781438479682 (pbk. : alk. paper) | ISBN 9781438479705
    (ebook)
Subjects: LCSH: Women—Political activity—New York (State)—History. |
    Women—Suffrage—New York (State)—History. | Feminism—New York
    (State)—History.
Classification: LCC HQ1236.5.U6 S84 2020 | DDC 320.082/09747—dc23
LC record available at https://lccn.loc.gov/2019032772

10 9 8 7 6 5 4 3 2 1

To the women of New York State—
past, present, and future

〰

CONTENTS

Part II: Interrogating the Present

Part III: Imagining the Future

ILLUSTRATIONS

Figures

Table

PREFACE

Introductory Remarks at Women in Politics: Past, Present, and Future

A Conference Commemorating the Centennial of Women's Suffrage in New York State

LIEUTENANT GOVERNOR KATHY HOCHUL

Women in New York won the right to vote in 1917, three years before the Nineteenth Amendment granted that right to women across the country. In order to commemorate this proud chapter of New York history, the state legislature and the governor created a Women's Suffrage Commission, which I have the honor of chairing. The commission was charged with organizing programs across the state to commemorate the centennial, beginning in 2017 and concluding in 2020. Looking back at the suffrage movement's history is certainly important, to honor the service of suffragist leaders and to learn from them. But it is not enough.

In fact, the mission of the Women's Suffrage Commission, as stated in law, is also to "help shape the future to ensure a more just and equitable society for all." While we remember and learn about our past, we cannot lose sight of the present and future. Of course, the common thread, from Seneca Falls in 1848 to this day, and in the years to come, is the simple belief that men and women should have equal rights. It's what suffragists fought for. It's what we fight for today when we talk about issues like equal pay for equal work and paid family leave.

Here in New York, we have the narrowest wage gap of any state: eighty-nine cents to the dollar. This positions us well to be the first state to eliminate the gap, but the gap is still there. Adding to that injustice is the fact that women of color fare worse than white women. Compared to white, non-Hispanic men, in New York, African American women are paid sixty-six cents on the dollar. Hispanic and Latina women are paid fifty-five cents on the dollar.

It's not accurate to say that the wage gap is a "women's issue." Women don't exist in a vacuum. When women make less than men, it doesn't only hurt them. It hurts their husbands, their wives, their partners, and their children. In New York State, 77 percent of single-parent families—that's more than six hundred thousand families—are headed by women. So when women are underpaid, their families—their children—suffer.

The wage gap also hurts our economy. A recent study by the New York Women's Foundation and the Institute for Women's Policy Research found that if we had equal pay for equal work, women in the state would earn about $6,600 more per year. This would add $29.6 billion to the state economy. Some studies have found that the United States could add up to $4.3 trillion in annual GDP in 2025 if women attain full gender equality.

I'm proud that the administration I am a part of has consistently taken bold actions toward eliminating the wage gap. New York State believes in leading by example. Many of the executive orders Governor Andrew Cuomo has signed concern employment practices in our own state agencies.

Paid family leave is another vital component in the struggle for gender equality. Governor Cuomo signed into law the most comprehensive paid family leave program in the nation.

The program will be transformational in terms of allowing people to care for a loved one—be it a new baby or an aging parent—in times of need. It will be especially transformational for women, because we know that women are still the primary caretakers. And while caretaking is important and noble, there's no question it affects your career, your earning potential. It even keeps some women out of the workforce altogether. Paid family leave applies equally to men and women, which is only logical.

Little by little, we can break down outdated gender roles and let men and women choose freely—without preconceived notions—how to divide caretaking responsibilities at home.

But how can we make sure that we continue to move forward toward equality?

I strongly believe the answer is in representation. Why aren't more women jumping into leadership roles—either as politicians or CEOs? Maybe it's because women hold themselves back. I am guilty of this; I did this to myself. When I was thirty-five years old, I served as counsel to Senator Daniel Patrick Moynihan. I had worked at a big law firm in Washington, DC. I had helped start several family businesses. I had children. I went to all the PTA meetings and school board meetings and town board meetings because I cared about my community. But at age thirty-five, I still did not think I had the qualifications to run for town board, even though nobody told me I couldn't.

I figured I would always be behind the scenes, always the staffer. I wrote the speeches. I came up with the ideas. And I was okay with that for way too long. I never viewed myself as being able to step up and speak before a crowd or have ideas that were worthy of enactment. I was just the person behind the scenes.

Then one day there was an opening on the town board and a twenty-two-year-old guy who had just graduated from college, was still living with his mom and dad, never had a job, had no mortgage, and didn't pay taxes raised his hand and said, "I want to run." That's when I thought, "Well, okay, maybe I've got something to offer, at least compared to that guy!"

Women do it all. We balance everything. We are masterful at running things. We can absolutely handle running a town or a county or a state or our country. We can figure out solutions and we can implement them. I say to women all around the state, "You are a twenty-two-year-old who cares about her community and cares about what is going on in America. Why aren't you thinking of yourself as a candidate? Why does a twenty-two-year-old man run for office but not a twenty-two-year-old woman?" Women all over this state, young and old, need to know that they have something to offer—and that they are just as capable, if not more so, than any man running for office.

In 2018, one hundred years after women in the state cast their first votes, we have to ask ourselves, a hundred years from now, what will our legacy be? We need to take the torch that was passed on

from the women of a century ago. This is how we will be judged—
not whether we kept the torch burning but whether we fanned the
flames against injustice and equality. Did we make it glow brighter
and stronger before we handed it off to the next generation? This is
our challenge.

ACKNOWLEDGMENTS

As editors, we must first thank the excellent contributors who were willing to join us in this book. We hope that the many hours they spent researching, writing, and revising will prove rewarding as this book reaches its audience. Special thanks go to our editor, Amanda Lanne-Camilli, for her patience and support, to production editor Jenn Bennett-Genthner, and to the editorial board at SUNY Press for believing in our project. As we prepared the manuscript, Martha Teck, SUNY New Paltz History Department secretary extraordinaire, devoted herself to the tedious task of transforming citations from historians, social scientists, and humanities scholars into a standard format. Colleagues and friends assisted by reading and commenting on drafts; special appreciation goes to Emily Hamilton-Honey, Susan Goodier, Ann F. Lewis, Scott Minkoff, Johanna Neuman, and Karen Pastorello. We acknowledge and appreciate our spouses (Richard, Matt, and Michael) for their enthusiastic encouragement and our children—grown (Rob, Ben, and Emily) and growing (Samuel and Jack)—for reminding us why these struggles matter. Finally, we thank each other for our collective hard work, happily balanced by our good humor and many lunches.

This book would not have been possible without the conference from which it developed: Women in Politics: Past, Present, and Future (April 21–22, 2017) held at the Franklin D. Roosevelt Presidential Library and Museum and SUNY New Paltz. The congenial and collaborative conference committee was chaired by Susan Lewis (History/ Women's, Gender, and Sexuality Studies Affiliate) and included Gerald Benjamin (Director, the Benjamin Center for Public Policy Initiatives); Kathleen Dowley (WGSS/Political Science); kt Tobin (Benjamin

Center/Sociology); Meg Devlin O'Sullivan (WGSS/History); Eve Walter (Benjamin Center/Sociology); Robin Jacobowitz (Benjamin Center); Dare Thompson (President, New York League of Women Voters); and Emily Vanderpool, Teresa Mandrin, and Jacklyn Greco (student interns). Particular thanks go to committee members Janis Benincasa (Benjamin Center), for her superb organizational abilities, and Christine Wilkins (Benjamin Center), for her attention to detail and positive attitude. We extend our deep gratitude to the conference committee members for their time, energy, and outstanding ideas.

We thank all of our conference collaborators, including the SUNY New Paltz Departments of History, Political Science, Sociology, and Women's, Gender, and Sexuality Studies; the Benjamin Center for Public Policy Initiatives at SUNY New Paltz; SUNY New Paltz Office of Academic Affairs; Friends of the Benjamin Center; the New York State League of Women Voters; the Franklin D. Roosevelt Presidential Library and Museum; the Hudson River Valley National Heritage Area; and the Nelson A. Rockefeller Institute of Government. Additional support was provided by the New York State Women's Suffrage Commission, the New York State Legislative Women's Caucus, Humanities New York, Mohonk Mountain House, Hudson River Valley Greenway, and Shmaltz Brewing Company. Sincere thanks go to the conference speakers, panelists, and presenters (see full program in the appendix) as well as everyone who attended—especially our students. Finally, the conference would never have happened without the leadership of Gerald Benjamin. Jerry organized the conference committee, identified key partners and brought them on board, and furnished the full support of the team at the Benjamin Center, who found sponsors and handled all of the conference's logistics.

Like suffrage itself, this book and the conference that produced it demanded the vision and efforts of many. We are indebted to you all.

INTRODUCTION

Suffrage and Its Limits

The New York Story

KATHLEEN M. DOWLEY, SUSAN LEWIS,
AND MEG DEVLIN O'SULLIVAN

This volume is the result of a two-day conference sponsored by
the Benjamin Center for Public Policy Initiatives at SUNY New
Paltz in collaboration with the New York State League of Women
Voters, the Franklin D. Roosevelt Presidential Library and Museum,
and the New York State Women's Suffrage Commission. The conference organizers sought to commemorate the centennial of woman
suffrage in New York State through a scholarly investigation of the
past, present, and future of women's social and political participation
and representation in state politics. The 2017 centennial of woman
suffrage at the state level offered a unique opportunity to examine
this watershed moment in the women's movement and New York
State history. Through a series of invited panels, presenters and
the audience engaged in an interdisciplinary and intergenerational
dialogue about the legacy and limits of suffrage, and its promise of
legal political equality, for women in New York. By bringing together
scholars from different regions of the state and across the country
with a wide variety of research specialties, the conference initiated a
dialogue between researchers, students, and the public that links an

understanding of past accomplishments to a clearer understanding of
present problems and an agenda for future progress.

When the conference organizing committee first met, we were
convinced of the timeliness of the topic—and assumed it would allow
us to make connections to the election of the first woman president.
That former New York senator Hillary Clinton did not achieve that
milestone suggests the questions asked and investigated here are still
relevant. At the time of the national centennial of woman suffrage,
and in the current political climate, perhaps they are even more urgent.

In her memoir *Woman Suffrage and Politics: The Inner Story of
the Suffrage Movement*, suffrage leader Carrie Chapman Catt wrote of
the movement:

> Hundreds of women gave the accumulated possibilities
> of an entire lifetime, thousands gave years of their lives,
> hundreds of thousands gave constant interest, and such
> aid as they could. It was a continuous, seemingly endless,
> chain of activity. Young suffragists who helped forge the
> last links of that chain were not born when it began, old
> suffragists who forged the first links were dead when it
> ended. . . . To them all its success became a monumental
> thing. (107–8)

The success, struggle, and victory about which Catt wrote was indeed
a monumental thing and well worth celebrating. Yet as we planned
for the conference and, subsequently, this volume, we aspired to
move beyond "celebrating" to commemorating and complicating this
history while connecting narratives of the past, present, and future
of New York State.

For us, commemorating meant taking seriously women's mobilization and political participation as a topic worthy of scholarly
investigation and debate. While we might have simply celebrated
that women were "given" the right to vote in New York in 1917,
we instead chose to commemorate the evidence that the vote was
not "given" to women, but fought for, over decades, by hundreds of
thousands of women, and many men, before it was finally won.

When we say that we wish to complicate, we argue for histories
that move beyond Seneca Falls, Elizabeth Cady Stanton, and Susan
B. Anthony. Although Stanton and Anthony are an important part

of the New York narrative we seek to understand, their story is not the only or even the central story of the New York (or national) centennial. The 1917 and 1920 centennials mark the anniversaries of what had become very different movements with different leaders, whose successful strategizing and organizing we seek to better understand in this volume.

We also endeavored to complicate our celebration by acknowledging some uncomfortable truths about many suffrage leaders and followers, including their nativism, classism, and racism. While acknowledging and confronting these truths does not negate their achievements, it allows us to interpret the past with greater clarity and honesty. When we do so, we can better connect the struggle for suffrage to later efforts to mobilize in defense of women's and civil rights and of struggles for racial justice. We can better understand some of the limits of such movements in our contemporary polarized political reality.

By making a conscious, collective effort to connect these mostly white, middle-class suffragists to the labor and efforts of African American, immigrant, working-class women who strove for the same goal, we complicate a "celebration" by acknowledging that the vote did not provide the panacea for women that many of the movement leaders thought it would. By recognizing that some women still struggle daily against sexism, racism, classism, settler colonialism, ableism, homophobia, transphobia, misogyny, and patriarchy, and therefore are denied effective voice in the political process, we query the notion that the struggle is over and complete victory achieved. Our book is organized in the manner of the conference, with nine chapters in total, three dedicated to the past, three to the present, and three to the future of women's social and political equality in New York and beyond. While all of the authors are established scholars in their respective fields, their presentations, from which the chapters are derived, were aimed at the non-expert audience, such as college undergraduates in a New York State history survey or a women and politics course, community members interested in suffrage and its limits, members of New York State and local historical societies, and educators in the region who wish to develop materials to teach the suffrage movement and will have every incentive to place New York in the context of this national conversation.

In part 1, "Investigating the Past," several historians reexamine the path to suffrage and its aftermath in New York State. In the first chapter, historians Susan Goodier and Karen Pastorello provide an in-depth investigation into the initial struggle for suffrage, from Seneca Falls through the early twentieth century. This chapter offers the necessary context for understanding Susan Ingalls Lewis's second chapter, which reviews current suffrage scholarship and asks why the movement succeeded in 1917 (having failed in 1915), focusing on the leadership strategies of Carrie Chapman Catt and Mary Garrett Hay. Finally, in the third installment on the past, Julie A. Gallagher, Joanna L. Grossman, and Meg Devlin O'Sullivan explore what happened in New York State and nationally after women won the vote, with particular attention to the experience of African American women in New York City, as voters, reformers, activists, and elected officials.

The next three chapters, "Interrogating the Present," focus on the current status of women and politics in New York State. In chapter 4, Kira Sanbonmatsu analyzes current levels and trends in women's representation in state politics, with an eye to comparing New York to other states. In chapter 5, kt Tobin provides newly collected data on women in local political offices in New York both to demonstrate that even at this oft-cited "entry" level, women lag behind men in executive-level positions and to identify continued obstacles in the gendered nature of some local political offices. Chapter 6 tackles the results of a survey designed to measure New Yorkers' attitudes about women and politics, funded by the Albany-based *Times Union* Women@Work initiative. Here Kathleen Dowley and Eve Walter confirm that although New York State remains a largely liberal "blue" state that votes for Democrats in the majority, gender gaps in public policy priorities persist.

Finally, in part 3, "Imagining the Future," a series of feminist writers reflect on the gains and limits of the suffrage movements for women going forward and the ongoing struggle for social, legal, and political equality in New York. In chapter 7, Amy Baehr lays out a robust defense of liberal feminism while identifying its central weakness in its failure to make "fairness" with regard to sharing in society's burdens (i.e., care work) as central as the demand for legal "rights" to its benefits (the vote, work, property). Jasmine Syedullah and Gabrielle Baron-Hill, in response to the charge to consider the "limits of liberal feminism and suffrage" for women, argue in chapter 8 that the limits of suffrage for gender equality is the unfinished work of abolition. In the final chapter, we present the conference keynote address of Barbara Smith, black feminist activist, author, and former two-term Albany council representative. Here Smith invites us to imagine a future informed by the lessons of organizing from the past.

PART I

INVESTIGATING THE PAST

Chapter 1

The Struggle for Suffrage and Its Aftermath in New York State

SUSAN GOODIER AND KAREN PASTORELLO

During a speech presented at the first annual convention of the American Equal Rights Association in New York City in 1867, Sojourner Truth, the most outspoken black feminist of her day, complained that discussions concerning the proposed Reconstruction amendments following the end of the Civil War ignored women. She elaborated: "I am glad to see that men are getting their rights, but I want women to get theirs . . . Now . . . is the time for women to step in." Truth's statement reveals the extraordinary promise of a social movement during a moment when working together to simultaneously end racial and gender discrimination in the United States Constitution seemed both logical and possible (Painter 1996, 220). The association, made up of women's rights activists and former abolitionists, demanded that Congress include women in the legislative changes that Reconstruction necessitated. Out of this association of black and white women and men came the organized suffrage movement, part of a complicated tapestry of civil rights activism that spanned decades. Although the universal promise of the American Equal Rights Association remains unfulfilled to the present day, it makes clear that the power to change the world lies in collaboration, cooperation, and working together despite dramatic differences.

The New York State woman suffrage story began in the decades following the American Revolution as part of an expansion of the republican ideals of liberty and equality for all. Women's rights activists faced monumental obstacles, not the least of which was the public attitude toward women's special sphere of influence (Kerber 1980, 11–12). While men dominated politics and political discourse in the public sphere, the "true womanhood" ideology required piety, purity, submission, and domesticity from women.[1] This ideology probably only applied to middle- and upper-class white women, and not to black, working-class, or immigrant women whose families could not afford to rely on one source of income. Yet promoters of this deeply rooted philosophy touted the necessity of gender separation for the health of society, rendering women's subordination critical to the proper functioning of the nation-state. This ideal, even if women did abide by it, did not confine women to the private sphere, however, as most people expected women to extend their responsibilities to include benevolence and charity work for those in need in their communities. New York State, predominantly rural, but on the cusp of the tremendous changes that would come with industrialization and increasing immigration, shaped the expectations for women over the next century.

Tracing the progress of the women's rights movement in New York illuminates the ways multifaceted groups of people dismantled formal and informal barriers that prevented women from full participation in the new democracy. By the 1840s, women activists demanded rights in social, legal, economic, and political arenas, with the vote as the "crowning jewel of individual freedom" (Du Bois 1998, 86). In 1846, six property-holding women in Jefferson County demanded the right, as taxpayers, to suffrage.[2] Two years later, the well-known Quaker abolitionist and minister Lucretia Mott of Philadelphia, her sister Martha Coffin Wright, and Quakers Jane Hunt and Mary Ann M'Clintock, along with Elizabeth Cady Stanton, organized a two-day women's rights conference in Seneca Falls.[3] The more than three hundred female and male attendees debated the Declaration of Sentiments, modeled on the Declaration of Independence, and ultimately accepted twelve resolutions. The strategies they proposed to attain their goals included educating women and the broader public about the need for women to enjoy more civil rights under the law, distributing and signing petitions, giving speeches, and writing tracts advocating for the recognition of increased property, marital, earning, social, and educational rights.[4] In essence, the resolutions would enable women to protect themselves and advance.

The cooperation between women's rights activists and abolitionists endured throughout the 1850s and into the 1860s. With the outbreak of the Civil War in 1861, women's rights activists suspended their annual women's rights conventions and set aside their reform goals to focus on the emancipation of enslaved people, founding the Women's National Loyal League to demand rights for African Americans (Tetrault 2014, 129). As these women displayed their patriotism, they also nursed wounded and dying soldiers in army hospitals, held sanitary fairs to raise money for the Union cause, and maintained the stability of their families while they ran farms and businesses. At the war's end in 1865, women's rights activists fully expected to be rewarded for their efforts in support of the Union (Free 2015, 133–61). Lucretia Mott, Martha Coffin Wright, Elizabeth Cady Stanton, Susan B. Anthony, Sojourner Truth, Ernestine Rose, Lucy Stone, Henry Blackwell, Frances Ellen Watkins Harper, and Matilda Joslyn Gage paid close attention as Congress discussed and debated the Fourteenth and Fifteenth Amendments.

In 1866, as Congress debated the wording of the amendments, abolitionists and women's rights activists established the American Equal Rights Association to demand suffrage for white and black women along with black men. With the venerable Lucretia Mott as president, the association drew prominent abolitionists and suffragists, black and white, such as Sojourner Truth, Frances Ellen Watkins Harper, Harriet Purvis, Robert Purvis, Sarah Remond, Frederick Douglass, William Lloyd Garrison, Samuel J. May, Stone, Blackwell, Anthony, Stanton, and others. All annual meetings took place in New York State, but speakers hailed from across the Northeast. The strategy of the association involved direct lobbying of legislators, primarily at the federal level; public lectures; and direct appeals for funding and support (Tetrault 2014, 20–30; DuBois 1978, 53–78). Hinting at disagreements among the leadership of the association, however, Stanton, Anthony, and Parker Pillsbury, with the backing of the racist but wealthy George Train, established the *Revolution*, a weekly newspaper to especially promote women's enfranchisement (Field 2014, 139–40). The *Revolution* stated in its first issue in 1868 that it would advocate "educated suffrage, irrespective of sex or color" (Stanton and Pillsbury 1868). The struggles of the association foreshadow some of the problems inherent in sustaining a cohesive woman suffrage movement until its ultimate success.

At the annual meeting held in New York City in May 1869, the American Equal Rights Association exploded over arguments about "how to achieve social transformation" (Tetrault 2014, 30). Some women and men urged support for the Fifteenth Amendment enfranchising only black men, while some women proposed a motion refusing to support the Fifteenth Amendment without an additional amendment enfranchising women. Charles C. Burleigh and Stephen Foster, both prominent white abolitionists, "wrested the control of the meeting" (Harper 1898, 1:324) from Susan B. Anthony and Elizabeth Cady Stanton, demanding that the amendment be accepted without continuing the agitation for women's enfranchisement until some unspecified time in the future (DuBois 1978, 186–91; Dudden 2011, 176–80; Goodier and Pastorello 2017, 12–13). Many women and men supported the amendment, but within days, Stanton, Anthony, and their colleague Matilda Joslyn Gage founded the National Woman Suffrage Association, headquartered in New York State, to focus on enfranchising women through an amendment to the federal constitution. The Bostonians Lucy Stone and her husband Henry Blackwell, both of whom supported the Fifteenth Amendment, countered by establishing the rival American Woman Suffrage Association, seeking state-by-state enfranchisement, in September. This maelstrom shaped the woman suffrage movement for the duration of its existence. Its basic characteristics defined a reform movement that generally ignored the rights of African Americans; a leadership of mostly white, middle-class women; and women's emancipation and equality primarily linked to their enfranchisement (DuBois 1978, 20). With the dissolution of the American Equal Rights Association, the leadership focused more specifically on the premise that all other rights women lacked would follow from their ability to vote (DuBois 1978, 54).

Gaining women's right to vote required broad acceptance. New York State eventually harbored tens of thousands of able, dedicated, energetic women who worked in rural and urban communities to persuade men to support votes for women. Forging a collaborative movement demanded the commitment of a loosely structured alliance of rural, immigrant, middle-class, radical, and black women from temperance, auxiliary, and women's clubs both upstate and downstate

(Goodier and Pastorello 2017, 3).[5] Well aware of the need to educate women about their lack of rights and their obligation to nurture the nation-state, suffragists urged support for women's direct participation in the polity.[6] However, the patriarchy of the dominant churches; the persistence of the separate spheres ideology; the reluctance of most men to relinquish social, legal, economic, and political power to women; and the notion that voting would interfere with their womanly responsibilities caused many women to resist the message of the movement. Susan B. Anthony and her biographer, the journalist Ida Husted Harper, saw it differently and claimed that "in the indifference, the inertia, the apathy of women, lies the greatest obstacle to their enfranchisement" (Anthony and Harper 1902, 2: xxiv). It was not that women did not want the vote; they did not know how much they needed it. The critical element was to convince their male relatives to vote for woman suffrage. The women of the broad coalition made progress by convincing their husbands, fathers, sons, and brothers of the rightness of women's voting rights.

To more effectively administer the activism of New York State suffragists, Matilda Joslyn Gage, a women's rights activist from Fayetteville, called a meeting of interested women and men at Congress Hall in Saratoga Springs in July 1869. Attendees established the New York State Woman Suffrage Association, which affiliated with the National Woman Suffrage Association. Arguing that denying the ballot to women contradicted the "genius of our institutions and the Declaration of Independence," they contended that taxation without representation was "base injustice," and considered the ballot to be the "legalized voice of the people" and the right of every law-abiding citizen of the state (Woman Suffrage Association of New York State, box 1, volume 1). The purpose of the organization, as stated in its constitution, was to demand the ballot for every woman of the state. They elected officers and convinced Martha Coffin Wright, who could not attend the meeting, to serve as the organization's first president. To encourage suffrage activism more broadly, members founded county-level suffrage clubs to oversee clubs in cities, towns, and villages in each of the (then) sixty counties of the state (Penney and Livingston 2003, 183; Penney and Livingston 2004, 186, 227; *Revolution*, February 4, 1869, 66).

Women engaged in the New York State woman suffrage movement, especially in rural areas, organized suffrage clubs, often called political equality clubs. Each club would make an annual dues payment of five dollars to affiliate with the state association. Clubs waxed and waned depending on the energies of the leaders. Some had as few as five members, while others, such as the Geneva Political Equality Club, counted approximately four hundred members by 1907. Thirty-six counties had clubs, representing over fifty-five thousand members, with Chautauqua County boasting over 1,800 members by the first decade of the twentieth century. During Harriet May Mills's tenure as association president (1910–1913), the number of political equality clubs virtually doubled, from approximately 250 in 1910 to 487 by 1914, "honeycomb[ing] the entire state with organizations" (New York Woman Suffrage Collection, 1914–15, box 1). The clubs began their work by securing women's right to vote for school board representatives, won in 1880, and moved on to advocating the same regarding tax questions in towns and villages. No matter how many issues club members addressed, and despite their constant struggle for money, woman suffrage remained the primary goal of all these clubs (Goodier and Pastorello 2017, 16, 34–36, 41). Club women worked to educate themselves on civil responsibilities, hosted suffrage schools to train speakers and organizers, attracted new members, printed and distributed literature, gathered signatures on petitions to the legislature, lobbied local politicians, published monthly newsletters, and forged liaisons between local, state, and national leadership (Mills 1901, 73).

The presidents of the New York State Woman Suffrage Association during the nineteenth century, in addition to Martha Coffin Wright (1869–1875), included Matilda Joslyn Gage (1875–1876, 1878), Susan B. Anthony (1876–1877), and Lillie Devereux Blake (1879–1890), all women with bold, dynamic, and broad visions for women's equality. During Gage's tenure, for example, she helped organize a centennial celebration at Philadelphia's Independence Hall. She procured rooms in the area, set about acquiring tickets to the celebration (she could only get five tickets as women were not really welcome), and drafted a "Declaration of Rights of Women." Gage, Anthony, Blake, attorney Phoebe Couzins, and college administrator Sarah Spencer interrupted the formal proceedings to submit this document to the assembly, shocking the men. The women then continued their celebrations out of doors, accompanied by members of the Hutchinson singers ("State Woman's Suffrage Association," n.d.; Stanton, Anthony, and Gage 1886, 11–44; Flexner and Fitzpatrick 1996, 163–64; Tetrault 2014,

99–102; National Woman Suffrage Association Centennial Album). The women kept an autograph book to record the names of visitors to the centennial headquarters and in September displayed the book in New York City, where Charlotte E. Ray, the first black woman lawyer in the United States, and many others signed it. Among the signatures appeared that of Sojourner Truth (National Woman Suffrage Association 1876 Centennial Autograph Book).

Religion dominated the lives of many woman suffragists, as it did the lives of most nineteenth-century Americans. Susan Fenimore Cooper, a devout Episcopalian, the daughter of novelist James Fenimore Cooper, and the acclaimed author of *Rural Hours* (1850), wrote "A Letter to the Christian Women of America" for *Harper's New Monthly Magazine* in 1870. She argued that women were historically and logically subordinate to men, that they were physically inferior, incapable of self-defense, and needed to trust in men's generosity for protection. Women were also intellectually inferior, "though in a very much less degree." No woman could call herself a Christian if she denied her subordinate role to men. Cooper, like the established Protestant church, contended that God decreed the role of women to be distinctly different from that of men. As an alternative to organized Christianity, a few suffragists subscribed to spiritualism, which "embraced" woman suffrage.[7] Some leading suffragists wrote controversial books claiming that most problems women faced were due to the patriarchy inherent in organized religion. Gage published *Woman, Church and State* in 1893, historicizing women's oppression. Two years later, Stanton, with the help of a committee of twenty-four American and European women's rights activists, came out with the first of two volumes of *The Woman's Bible*, revising the Bible to confront the orthodoxy of the Christian churches. However, Cooper articulated reasons for opposing women's enfranchisement that persisted for the next fifty years.

Religious or not, rural women, many of whom understood their hard work and contributions to family farms as critical to the stability of society, found suffrage arguments appealing. The lack of political rights rankled property-owning farm women. As Grange member and temperance supporter Ella Goodell reasoned, the vote would "benefit overworked farm women" (Marti 1991, 7, 111–14). Leadership in the Grange movement encouraged women to claim their rights in the broader political sphere. Eliza Gifford, a state-level Grange leader and vice president of the Jamestown Political Equality Club, believed that "humanity can never be capable of its greatest achievements until the wife and mother takes her proper place beside her husband, his co-equal and helpmate" (Cutter 1912, 1127). Rural women provided the foundation for the broad dissemination of suffrage ideology despite numerous obstacles and the isolation they faced. Many of the women who rose to prominence in the state suffrage movement came from rural communities.

New York suffrage leadership, however, often resided and campaigned in urban areas. Lillie Devereux Blake, for example, found several ways to challenge the patriarchy. She and her supporters relentlessly campaigned against Lucius Robinson—the governor who refused to sign into law a bill allowing women to vote in school elections—by writing letters, publishing circulars, and making speeches. After Alonzo B. Cornell, Robinson's opponent, won the governorship, he satisfied suffragists by signing the legislation on February 15, 1880 (Stanton, Anthony, and Gage 1886, 417, 422–23; Farrell 2002, 152–53). Many women voted in school elections, although some found their visits to the polling places unwelcome. In 1886, the New York State Woman Suffrage Association protested the unveiling and dedication of the Statue of Liberty. Although not invited to the celebrations, suffragists rented a cattle barge (which lacked even basic comforts) and went out into the harbor to protest the fact that France had gifted a statue, representing liberty, to a country where no women had liberty (Wagner 1992, 111–14; Farrell 2002, 155). During her tenure, Blake especially focused her efforts on lobbying the legislature to test the reach of women's political power, a strategy that often put her in opposition to Anthony.

Hester Jeffrey, a friend of Susan B. Anthony, dominated black women's suffrage activism in Rochester, but increasingly white women did not welcome African American women to their meetings and events. Although there is some evidence that they attended women's rights conventions, black women began to establish their own organizations for woman suffrage. Sarah Smith Tompkins Garnet and several of her friends and teaching colleagues founded the Colored Woman's Suffrage League of Brooklyn in the late 1880s (Wellman 2014, 128). Usually, the African Methodist Episcopal Church formed the locus of black women's suffrage activism across the state. They virtually never separated agitation for the right to vote from their other needs. These educated and financially stable women broadly engaged in social justice work, much of which was directed at anti-lynching, abolishing racism and discrimination, and racial uplift. For example, members regularly sent money to support Harriet Tubman's home for the aged in Auburn and raised funds for a Frederick Douglass memorial in Rochester.[8]

While women demanded a wide range of reform goals in their organized movement, by the end of the nineteenth century the controversial call for women's elective franchise became their most intense focus. Women came to see the vote as the route to full democratic participation, at the same time realizing that, as historian Ellen Carol DuBois (1978, 46) notes, "the suffrage demand challenged the idea that women's interests were identical or even compatible with men's." They understood that men could not speak for them. As the movement progressed, women refined their rhetoric and developed their activist talents. By 1889, Anthony and Alice Stone Blackwell, the daughter of Lucy Stone and Henry Blackwell, began negotiations to merge the National Woman Suffrage Association and the American Woman Suffrage Association (Tetrault 2014, 161). Many members strongly opposed the merger; Gage argued that the parties involved violated the National Association's governing constitution. In addition, members of the two associations still differed on overall strategy (federal amendment as opposed to state-by-state enfranchisement), and they disagreed about the value of partial as opposed to full suffrage (Tetrault 2014, 156–61).

The National American Woman Suffrage Association (NAWSA), established at a convention held in Washington, DC, in February 1890, became more centralized and hierarchical in its structure. The most mainstream of all the suffrage organizations, NAWSA expanded its base more broadly by drawing in the "evangelical" Woman's Christian Temperance Union (Tetrault 2014, 165). Gage, arguing that "the full extent of the treachery by which we were sold has not yet been fathomed," left the newly formed organization and founded another to focus on the separation of church and state (Wagner 1998, 53). The need to appeal to a broader segment of the population also affected the New York State movement, apparent in the transition from Blake as president to the installation of the more moderate Jean Brooks Greenleaf.

During Greenleaf's tenure, in preparation for a New York State Constitutional Convention in 1894, Anthony, Carrie Chapman Catt, Mary Walker, Anna Howard Shaw, Mary Putnam Jacobi, and many other suffrage activists traveled across the state to educate people about the intention of legislators to discuss the removal of the word "male" as a descriptor of "voter" in the constitution (Hamlin 1990, 255; Harper 1898, 2:760–61; Shaw 1915, 245). Women who opposed political enfranchisement, at first called remonstrants, realized that unless they publicly stated their position, there was a real possibility that voting would be added to their duties. So at the same time women suffragists aggressively campaigned in nearly every one of the state's sixty counties, anti-suffragists met in upstate city parlors or at the Waldorf Hotel in New York City. They formed temporary committees to discuss women's proper role in the polity, write articles, distribute literature, and collect signatures on petitions resisting enfranchisement.

While convention delegates ultimately voted not to submit the question to the electorate, anti-suffragists eventually found it expedient to establish permanent organizations to counteract the efforts of suffragists. Organized anti-suffragists, usually drawn from the same socioeconomic status as suffragists, actually helped suffragists to more precisely craft their arguments. Founded in 1895, the New York State Association Opposed to Woman Suffrage, led by women such as Lucy Parkman Scott, Abby Hamlin Abbott, and Josephine Jewell Dodge, coordinated the state and national opposition to women gaining the right to vote until 1911, when anti-suffragists established the National Association Opposed to Woman Suffrage and elected Dodge as president. Thereafter, Alice Hill Chittenden served as president of the New York State Association. Eventually, elite men formed the Men's League Opposed to Woman Suffrage, drawing on the women's financial resources and administrative talents.[9]

By the turn of the century, supporters of the state suffrage organization strove to broaden the appeal of woman suffrage. The presidents of the New York Association following Greenleaf (1890–1896) included Marianna Wright Chapman (1896–1902), Ella Hawley Crossett (1902–1910), Harriet May Mills (1910–1913), Gertrude Foster Brown (1913–1915), and Vira Boarman Whitehouse (1915–1917). In 1909, during Crossett's tenure, the headquarters for the state association moved from Mills's home in Syracuse to a Fifth Avenue office building in New York City to increase suffrage visibility and outreach (Hoffert 2012, 76). Sharing headquarters with the National American Woman Suffrage Association, state suffragists relied on guidance from its leadership, particularly that of Carrie Chapman Catt. Many women, including Crossett, Elnora Babcock (of the Chautauqua Political Equality Club, who coordinated press work for both the state and national organizations), and Emily Howland (Cayuga County women's rights activist, reformer of African American education, and major financial contributor), also served as delegates to national conventions.[10] Drawing on diverse talents and energy, and using every resource available to them, including Catt's expertise, New York State suffrage leaders systemized their activities, centrally coordinated their outreach, and created a disciplined organization poised for the state suffrage victory.

To appeal to working women, Catt and Harriot Stanton Blatch (Elizabeth Cady Stanton's daughter) reached out to Charlotte Perkins Gilman, Florence Kelley, and other labor rights proponents, such as those who held membership in the Women's Trade Union League. Susan B. Anthony and many of her colleagues had long believed that political empowerment would increase wages, shorten working hours, alleviate unsafe workplace and living conditions, and open advancement opportunities for working women (Anthony [1871] 1981, 139–45; Flexner 1996, 133–37). As immigrant women entered the industrial workforce in unprecedented numbers, Lillian Wald and other settlement house workers provided services to help them and their families, thereby drawing immigrants into the realm of suffrage and political activism. Black women such as Victoria Earle Matthews and Verina Morton Jones sought to provide parallel services and opportunities through institutions like the White Rose Mission and the Lincoln Settlement House (Goodier and Pastorello 2017, 73, 81, 83–84). After the horrific 1911 Triangle Shirtwaist Factory fire exposed the raw realities of immigrant women's working lives, activists such as Margaret Hinchey and Leonora O'Reilly traveled across the state to promote civil engagement and government intervention to solve the problems of urban immigrant women. Others such as Katherine Dreier reiterated these ideas to multiple ethnic groups in New York City (Woman Suffrage Association of New York State, box 9, volume 6). Progressive Era suffrage activists touted the vote as a panacea able to solve women's social, legal, and economic problems.

Increasingly, men agreed with them. Frederick Douglass, Unitarian minister Samuel J. May, and prominent businessman Maurice Leyden—who, with his wife and Anthony, had campaigned for women's enfranchisement throughout Rochester—had supported woman suffrage since the inception of the movement.[11] When Anna Howard Shaw encouraged *New York Post* editor Oswald Garrison Villard, son

of suffragist and civil rights activist Fannie Garrison Villard, to found
a men's organization in the early twentieth century, it helped make
women's enfranchisement seem even more acceptable. The most
motivated male supporters lived with mothers, sisters, lovers, or wives
in households replete with suffrage sentiment. By 1908, Columbia
University graduate student Max Eastman, along with the support
of the widely respected Rabbi Stephen S. Wise, launched the Men's
League for Woman Suffrage. Men's League members heightened suffrage
visibility through lobbying efforts in Albany and by marching behind
women in parades to show support rather than direction, acting in
pageants, hosting dinners, speaking at woman suffrage events, raising
money, and publicly endorsing suffrage for women. While men's level
of commitment to suffrage never rivaled women's, their efforts encouraged more men than ever before to endorse women's right to vote.
It would be their ballots, after all, that would enfranchise women.

Twentieth-century suffragists made woman suffrage fashionable,
popular, and reasonable by brilliantly marketing their cause. Suffragists overlooked no consumer goods in their quest to promote their
movement, deliberately influencing fashion, art, postcards, parades,
and pageants, as well as making use of every form of transportation,
including automobiles, trains, trolleys, boats, and airplanes.[12] When war
broke out in Europe in August 1914, suffragists marketed patriotism
along with woman suffrage. Although the United States sought to
remain neutral, many pro- and anti-suffrage women worked together
as they engaged in war preparedness activities. Observers criticized
suffragists for continuing to advance their cause during this period,
but most activists wove the promotion of suffrage into their war work.
For example, as women like Westchester County suffragist Narcissa
Cox Vanderlip and members of the New York City Committee on
National Defense knocked on doors to canvass for the war effort,
or sold government bonds, they wore their suffrage pins, distributed
suffrage literature, and discussed women's need for the vote (Goodier
and Pastorello 2017, 152–57). Despite the distraction of the war,
and unlike their anti-suffrage counterparts who neglected suffrage to
engage in war-related work, suffrage campaigners continued to focus
on their push for women's enfranchisement.

During the Empire State Campaign (1913–1915), suffragists
distributed over one million pieces of "Vote Yes" literature in multiple languages, posting it in store windows, post offices, and county

fair booths. In a September 1915 letter to assembly district leaders, Empire State Campaign leader Carrie Chapman Catt also encouraged them to hold rallies and address audiences in towns and villages in their districts, her organizational strategy utilized in the state since 1907 (Catt Papers). Suffrage discussions and events dominated social calendars, filled newspaper columns, attracted crowds to suffragists' parades, and permeated Sunday sermons and the Chautauqua summer lecture circuit. The German American [suffrage] Committee donated money to the cause, held fund-raising dinners, and hosted its own contingent in the "Monster Suffrage Parade" held in October 1915 (New York Public Library Organization Papers, box 2, folder 9; Woman Suffrage Association of New York State, box 7, volume 8). Everyone everywhere had something to say about woman suffrage. The 1915 ballot, offered during a midterm election year, listed five amendments regarding constitutional changes involving language, finance, apportionment, and taxes, and for the first time presented the question of removing the word "male" from the definition of a citizen. Only the rural counties of Chautauqua, Chemung, Schenectady, Broome, and Tompkins passed the referendum. Suffragists, although distressed at the loss, felt some optimism when they realized that of 1.3 million votes cast, five hundred thousand men did not vote on the suffrage issue at all. Suffrage activists believed they could convince those men to vote for woman suffrage by the next referendum, and they immediately began the process necessary to place the referendum on the next ballot.

By 1916, women implemented the lessons they had learned during the Empire State Campaign, hosting more suffrage schools and following up all their canvassing efforts with education. Suffrage leaders reaffirmed the necessity of convincing men—regardless of their ethnicity, race, socioeconomic class, political persuasion, or place of residence—of the justice of woman suffrage. New York suffragists received a boon when the courts finally settled the estate of Mrs. Frank Leslie. Its beneficiary, Carrie Chapman Catt, presented $10,000 to Vira Boarman Whitehouse for the upstate campaign and gifted $15,000 to Mary Garrett Hay, president of the Woman Suffrage Party and the New York Equal Suffrage League, for her efforts in New York City (Young 1929, 59–62, 91). The Colored Woman's Suffrage Club of New York City and other black women's groups, although critical of the tendency of white women to discriminate against them, expanded their efforts to reach voters at the same time (New York Age 1917, 1).

Meanwhile, the war continued to preempt suffrage news. The conundrum of fighting a war to "make the world safe for democracy" made it increasingly obvious that women reaped no benefits from citizenship. More than sixty New York women, along with hundreds of other women from across the United States, picketed the White House. Many spent time in jail, some suffering brutal punishments or force-feeding.[13] The New York State Woman Suffrage Association, like the National American Woman Suffrage Association, did not commit its resources to the war effort until February 1917. In April, the United States finally entered the war. Suffragists then targeted soldiers and sailors both by canvassing them in training camps and by volunteering their services to mail absentee ballots to men serving overseas. Their war-related efforts normalized the idea that women could play a dynamic role in the government and in making political decisions, and some high government officials began to consider woman suffrage as a war measure. Bowing to the pressure of the energetic Mary Garrett Hay, Tammany Hall withdrew its opposition and on November 6, 1917, nearly 54 percent of state voters approved the right of women to vote (Baker 1991, 144–47).

The New York State woman suffrage movement drew its membership and support from a wide spectrum of the population. As the decades passed, suffrage activists frequently created new strategies to revitalize the image and message of the movement. While it counted elites among its essential leadership and membership, and the activities of elites fascinated the media, they remained in the minority. Elite women did not have power over the majority of male voters; they needed women from the diverse masses upstate and downstate to influence their male relatives and friends. Ultimately, woman suffrage required a coalition of supporters from across the socioeconomic spectrum to succeed, although some elite white women would have excluded black or immigrant women from the franchise if they could have (Goodier and Pastorello 2017, 3, 194). Even after the referendum passed, Native American women (and men), still not granted the privileges of citizenship, could not vote. Despite the movement's legacy of racism and exclusion, the cross-cultural, cross-class, cross-race alliances of these extraordinary women held great promise. Significantly, once New York women won their enfranchisement, they shifted their considerable resources and energies to secure a federal amendment. As Carrie Chapman Catt had once put it, "It is a blessed privilege to labor for suffrage in the Empire State for when New York is won the United States is won; when the United States is won, the civilized world will soon follow" (Catt Papers).

Notes

1. For more on the "true womanhood" or separate spheres ideology, see Welter (1963), Kraditor (1970), and Cott (1997, xi–xxvii). More recently, scholars have challenged and refined the usefulness of the ideology; see, for example, Landes (2003).

2. For more on this petition, see Ginzberg (2005).

3. DuBois (1978, 26).

4. For a detailed account of the convention, see Wellman (2004, 193–208).

5. Tetrault (2014, 47–51) points out that the national suffrage movement also had intersecting and disparate goals, strategies, and leaders.

6. The argument that women had something unique to offer the nation-state is articulated in Kraditor (1965, 38–63).

7. Quakers, or the Society of Friends, a Christian sect, allowed women more active roles in their religious activities. It is probable that Cooper did not consider Quaker women in her definition of Christian women (Goldsmith 1998, 48–49).

8. For more on African American women's suffrage efforts, see Terborg-Penn (1998); Gallagher (2014); and Goodier and Pastorello (2017), especially chapter 4.

9. For more on the anti-suffrage movement in New York State, see Goodier (2013).

10. For more on Elnora Babcock and the Political Equality Movement in Chautauqua, see Babcock (1904); for more on Emily Howland, see Breault (1976) and Woman Suffrage Association of New York State (box 9).

11. For more on Leyden, see Miles (2005).

12. For more on the suffrage influence on consumerism, see Finnegan (1999) and Florey (2013, 2015).

13. For more about protesting at the White House during World War I, see Stevens (1995) and Zahniser and Fry (2014).

Works Cited

Anthony, Susan B. (1871) 1981. "Suffrage and the Working Woman." In *Elizabeth Cady Stanton, Susan B. Anthony: Correspondence, Writings,*

Speeches, edited and with a critical commentary by Ellen Carol DuBois, 139–45. New York: Schocken Books.

Anthony, Susan B., and Ida Husted Harper, eds. 1902. *History of Woman Suffrage*. Vol. 4 (1883–1900). Indianapolis, IN: Hollenbeck Press.

Babcock, Elnora Monroe. 1904. "Political Equality Movement." In *The Centennial History of Chautauqua County, New York*, vol. 1, 510–19. Jamestown, NY: Chautauqua History Company. https://archive.org/stream/centennialhistor01chau#page/510/mode/2up.

Baker, Paula. 1991. *The Moral Frameworks of Public Life: Gender, Politics, and the State in Rural New York, 1870–1930*. New York: Oxford University Press.

Breault, Judith Colucci. 1976. *The World of Emily Howland: Odyssey of a Humanitarian*. Millbrae, CA: Les Femmes.

Catt, Carrie Chapman. Papers. Correspondence Files, Empire State Campaign Committee. Bryn Mawr College Archives.

Cott, Nancy F. 1997. *The Bonds of Womanhood: "Woman's Sphere" in New England, 1780–1835*. 2nd ed. New Haven, CT: Yale University Press.

Cutter, William Richard, ed. 1912. *Genealogical and Family History of Western New York: A Record of the Achievement of Her People in the Making of a Commonwealth in the Building of a Nation*. Vol. 3. New York: Lewis Historical.

DuBois, Ellen Carol. 1978. *Feminism and Suffrage: The Emergence of an Independent Women's Movement in America, 1848–1869*. Ithaca, NY: Cornell University Press.

———. 1998. *Woman Suffrage and Women's Rights*. New York: New York University Press.

Dudden, Faye E. 2011. *Fighting Chance: The Struggle over Woman Suffrage and Black Suffrage in Reconstruction America*. New York: Oxford University Press.

Farrell, Grace. 2002. *Lillie Devereux Blake: Retracing a Life Erased*. Amherst: University of Massachusetts Press.

Field, Corrine T. 2014. *The Struggle for Equal Adulthood: Gender, Race, Age, and the Fight for Citizenship in Antebellum America*. Chapel Hill: University of North Carolina Press.

Finnegan, Margaret. 1999. *Selling Suffrage: Consumer Culture and Votes for Women*. New York: Columbia University Press.

Flexner, Eleanor, and Ellen Fitzpatrick. 1996. *Century of Struggle: The Woman's Rights Movement in the United States*. Cambridge, MA: Belknap Press of Harvard University Press.

Florey, Kenneth. 2013. *Women's Suffrage Memorabilia: An Illustrated Historical Study*. Jefferson, NC: McFarland.

———. 2015. *American Woman Suffrage Postcards: A Study and Catalog*. Jefferson, NC: McFarland.

Free, Laura E. 2015. *Suffrage Reconstructed: Gender, Race, and Voting Rights in the Civil War Era*. Ithaca, NY: Cornell University Press.

Gage, Matilda Joslyn. 1893. *Woman, Church and State*. 2nd ed. New York: Truth Seeker. http://www.sacred-texts.com/wmn/wcs/index.htm.

Gallagher, Julie A. 2014. *Black Women and Politics in New York City*. Urbana: University of Illinois Press.

Ginzberg, Lori D. 2005. *Untidy Origins: A Story of Woman's Rights in Antebellum New York*. Chapel Hill: University of North Carolina Press.

Goldsmith, Barbara. 1998. *Other Powers: The Age of Suffrage, Spiritualism, and the Scandalous Victoria Woodhull*. New York: Alfred A. Knopf.

Goodier, Susan. 2013. *No Votes for Women: The New York State Anti-Suffrage Movement*. Urbana: University of Illinois Press.

Goodier, Susan, and Karen Pastorello. 2017. *Women Will Vote: Winning Suffrage in New York State*. Ithaca, NY: Cornell University Press.

Hamlin, Huybertie Pruyn. 1990. *An Albany Girlhood*. Edited by Alice P. Kenney. Albany, NY: Washington Park Press.

Harper, Ida Husted. 1898. *The Life and Work of Susan B. Anthony*. 2 vols. Indianapolis, IN: Hollenbeck Press.

Hoffert, Sylvia D. 2012. *Alva Vanderbilt Belmont: Unlikely Champion of Women's Rights*. Bloomington: Indiana University Press.

Kerber, Linda. 1980. *Women of the Republic: Intellect and Ideology in Revolutionary America*. Chapel Hill: University of North Carolina Press.

Kraditor, Aileen S. 1965. *Ideas of the Woman Suffrage Movement, 1890–1920*. New York: Columbia University Press.

———. 1970. *Up from the Pedestal: Selected Writings in the History of American Feminism*. Chicago: Quadrangle Books.

Landes, Joan B. 2003. "Further Thoughts on the Public/Private Distinction." *Journal of Women's History* 15, no. 2 (Summer): 28–39.

Marti, Donald B. 1991. *Women of the Grange: Mutuality and Sisterhood in Rural America, 1866–1920*. Westport, CT: Greenwood Press.

Miles, Randall. 2005. "The Maurice Leyden Collection: Scope and Content." Binghamton University Special Collections. https://www.binghamton.edu/libraries/special-collections/researchandcollections/findingaids/civilwar/Leyden_FA.pdf.

Mills, Harriet May. 1901. Newsletter, March 1901, Scrapbook 3. Miller National American Woman Suffrage Association Scrapbooks, 1897–1911. Rare Book and Special Collections Division, Library of Congress.

National Woman Suffrage Association 1876 Centennial Autograph Book. Onondaga Historical Association, Syracuse, NY.

New York Age. 1917. "Suffragists Drew No Line." September 20, 1917.

New York Woman Suffrage Collection, 1914–15. Collection 8041. Division of Rare and Manuscript Collections, Carl A. Kroch Library, Cornell University.

Painter, Nell Irvin. 1996. *Sojourner Truth: A Life, a Symbol.* New York: W. W. Norton.

Penney, Sherry H., and James D. Livingston. 2003. "Getting to the Source: Hints for Wives—and Husbands." *Journal of Women's History* 15, no. 2 (Summer): 180–87.

———. 2004. *A Very Dangerous Woman: Martha Wright and Women's Rights.* Amherst: University of Massachusetts Press.

Shaw, Anna Howard. 1915. *The Story of a Pioneer.* New York: Harper Brothers.

Stanton, Elizabeth Cady. 1898. *The Woman's Bible.* New York: European. http://www.sacred-texts.com/wmn/wb/wb00.htm.

Stanton, Elizabeth Cady, Susan B. Anthony, and Matilda Joslyn Gage, eds. 1886. *History of Woman Suffrage.* Vol. 3. Rochester, NY: Susan B. Anthony.

Stanton, Elizabeth Cady, and Parker Pillsbury, eds. 1868. "The Revolution Will Advocate." *Revolution,* January 8, 1868, 1.

Stevens, Doris. 1995. *Jailed for Freedom: American Women Win the Vote.* Edited by Carol O'Hare. Troutdale, OR: New Sage Press. First published 1920.

Terborg-Penn, Rosalyn. 1998. *African American Women in the Struggle for the Vote, 1850–1920.* Bloomington: Indiana University Press.

Tetrault, Lisa. 2014. *The Myth of Seneca Falls: Memory and the Women's Suffrage Movement, 1848–1898.* Chapel Hill: University of North Carolina Press.

Wagner, Sally Roesch. 1992. *A Time of Protest: Suffragists Challenge the Republic: 1870–1887.* Aberdeen, SD: Sky Carrier Press.

———. 1998. *Matilda Joslyn Gage: She Who Holds the Sky.* Aberdeen, SD: Sky Carrier Press.

Wellman, Judith. 2004. *The Road to Seneca Falls: Elizabeth Cady Stanton and the First Woman's Rights Convention.* Urbana: University of Illinois Press.

———. 2014. *Brooklyn's Promised Land: The Free Black Community of Weeksville, New York.* New York: New York University Press.

Welter, Barbara. 1966. "The Cult of True Womanhood, 1820–1860." *American Quarterly* 18, no. 2 (Summer): 151–74.

Woman Suffrage Association of New York State. Records, 1869–1919. Collection 1369. Rare Book and Manuscript Library, Butler Library, Columbia University.

Young, Rose. 1929. *The Record of the Leslie Woman Suffrage Commission, Inc., 1917–1929.* New York: Leslie Woman Suffrage Commission.

Zahniser, J. D., and Amelia R. Fry. 2014. *Alice Paul: Claiming Power.* New York: Oxford University Press.

Chapter 2

1917

How New York Women Won the Vote

SUSAN INGALLS LEWIS[1]

The year 2017 marked the centennial of women winning the right to vote in New York State—an opportunity to memorialize a vital turning point in United States history. Previously, it seemed that most Americans, even most New Yorkers, assumed that all women in the United States had been granted suffrage at the same time, as the result of the Nineteenth Amendment to the US Constitution passed in 1920. Actually, women won the vote across the nation in an irregular, piecemeal fashion. The territory of Wyoming allowed women to vote in 1869 and, when it became a state in 1890, was the first state where women could vote in all elections. By the time the federal suffrage amendment was passed, fifteen states (including New York) already had full suffrage and many others had partial suffrage—that is, women could vote in some but not all elections. For example, in some states or localities women could vote in presidential elections, primaries, municipal elections, or school board elections.

The centennial provided an excellent opportunity to explore important questions about how and why New York was the first state east of the Mississippi in which women won the elective franchise. Among many possible historical questions, these stood out: (1) why the referendum to give women equal suffrage passed in 1917, not earlier or later; (2) why New York (rather than another eastern state)

27

was the first to confirm voting as a woman's right; and (3) which individuals, groups, and tactics were most responsible for the New York suffrage victory.

Most important, the suffrage centennial commemorations in New York offered a unique opening to move into new historical territory. Instead of retracing old ground and reinscribing former myths, this was a chance to stress the importance of those who were truly central to New York's final suffrage victory, individuals like Carrie Chapman Catt, Mary Garret Hay, Harriot Stanton Blatch, Alva Vanderbilt Belmont, Vira Boarman Whitehouse, Rose Schneiderman, Mary Burnett Talbert, and many more. It also enabled the historical community to present to the press, the public, and our students recent scholarship and historical analysis, insights that go far beyond idealized images, mythology, and well-known iconic figures. The centennial also inspired outstanding exhibitions at the New York State Museum (*Votes for Women: Celebrating New York's Suffrage Centennial*, with a companion book by Jennifer Lemak and Ashley Hopkins-Benton [2017]) and the Museum of the City of New York (*Beyond Suffrage: A Century of New York Women in Politics*).

Yet, disappointingly, public events and reading lists extolling the contributions of Susan B. Anthony, Elizabeth Cady Stanton, Sojourner Truth, and Matilda Joslyn Gage (all of whom were dead more than a decade before 1917) seemed more common than those analyzing the successful tactics of 1917 or the individuals who shaped that victory.[2] It was as if a celebration of the civil rights movement of the 1960s ignored the strategy of nonviolent resistance and neglected Martin Luther King in favor of honoring Frederick Douglass.

Sadly, Anthony, Stanton, Truth, and Gage were all important leaders who ultimately failed to see their dreams fulfilled—not for lack of energy or compelling arguments, but because they were unable to convince most male legislators and voters of their period that women needed or deserved the vote. Even the majority of women in the United States were probably not persuaded that enfranchising women was vitally important at the time that the most iconic of these figures, Anthony, died in 1906. (Stanton had died in 1902, Gage in 1898, and Truth in 1883.) Most surprising to many today (as described by Goodier [2013] in her monograph *No Votes for Women: The New York State Anti-Suffrage Movement*), there was actually a strong anti-suffrage movement led by New York women.

This essay presents an opportunity to delve into historical material and complicate arguments that, despite the opportunity created by the state and national centennials, remain underexplored in public and political discourse. The latest scholarship on New York's suffrage victory represents both painstaking research and sophisticated analysis, but recent work has not yet filtered into public knowledge. Although the centennial is now past us, I would argue for the continued importance of studying the New York suffrage story. A detailed narrative tracing the history of the suffrage movement within New York State can be found in Susan Goodier and Karen Pastorello's excellent, meticulously researched essay in this volume, and in their monograph on the same topic, *Women Will Vote* (Goodier and Pastorello 2017). This chapter will review current scholarship on the successful New York suffrage campaign and offer a range of interpretations of the factors that led to the final victory.

Background: The Progressive Era and the "New Woman"

The period from 1848 to 1920 is commonly known as the "first wave" of the feminist movement, but that term gives a false impression of unity. What was called the "woman" movement by its participants changed over time in both focus and tactics, and within each period participants often differed about which goals to pursue and how to accomplish them. The Progressive Era (1890–1920) was a pivotal period for many reform movements. The suffrage victory was clearly a product of this historical moment, which was distinguished by remarkable female activism and major changes in American women's roles and expectations, as well as dramatic developments in the women's movement itself.

In 1890, the two major women's rights organizations (the National Woman Suffrage Association and the American Woman Suffrage Association), which had split the movement after the Civil War (see preceding essay), united to form the National American Woman Suffrage Association (NAWSA). Under the leadership of Susan B. Anthony, NAWSA became the major US organization promoting women's voting rights. At the same time, woman suffrage also gained support from other reform groups, most notably the Women's Christian

Temperance Union (WCTU) under Frances Willard. Temperance, a movement devoted to limiting or abolishing the consumption of alcohol in the United States, was supported by many women because male alcoholism was associated with spousal abuse and the neglect of family responsibilities. The support of the WCTU was a huge advantage for NAWSA in terms of membership (far more women had been committed to temperance than to suffrage), but it stiffened the resistance of liquor manufacturers and immigrant communities to women's voting rights, and it alienated suffragists committed to the separation between church and state, like Matilda Joslyn Gage.

Another vital development of the 1890s was the emergence of a new model of ideal womanhood, the so-called "New Woman." In direct contrast to the archetypical Victorian maiden or matron, the "New Woman" was independent, educated, self-supporting, and often professional (Patterson 2005, 2008). The typical "New Woman" fought for suffrage but also for many other causes. She might live and work in a settlement house (like Jane Addams), serve as a factory inspector and expose the plight of child laborers (like Florence Kelley), advocate for birth control (like Margaret Sanger), campaign against lynching (like Ida B. Wells), organize women workers (like Rose Schneiderman), head a woman's association dedicated to racial uplift (like Mary Church Terrell), or simply work as a journalist, writer, teacher, lawyer, public health nurse, doctor, or minister. "New Women" (who included those of diverse races, religions, classes, and national origins) were at the heart of the Progressive movement, in New York State as well as across the country. As the first generation of women's rights trailblazers reached the end of their lives, leadership of the suffrage movement passed to such "New Women," born shortly before, during, and after the Civil War, and often college-educated professionals.

Interestingly, the argument for women's voting rights also changed somewhat between the mid-nineteenth and early twentieth centuries. Anthony, Stanton, and Gage, as well as Truth and other suffragists of color like Frances Harper, had argued that women deserved the vote as a human right. The "New Women" of the early twentieth century added the justification that women deserved the vote not just because they were like men but also because they were different and represented different ideals that would benefit the state. These women argued that females were by nature more caring, more peaceful, more nurturing, and more selfless than men, and that they would bring better values into the political process, reforming government for men, women, and children alike. Yet suffragists never abandoned the issue of equality; instead of seeing these arguments as contradictory, they saw them as mutually supportive.

This generation of suffrage activists not only brought a fresh energy to the movement but devised tactics that were more public, dramatic, and commercial than the speeches, petition drives, and educational efforts of the past. Unafraid of "displaying themselves" (despite public criticism) on street corners and in parades, they harnessed the power of the mass media and advertising to support their cause.

Analysis of the 1917 Victory:
Who Was Responsible?

One's historical interpretation of the 1917 New York State referendum victory depends to a large extent on one's understanding of how social movements succeed. Emphasizing Stanton's and Anthony's leadership, for example, suggests that the most important aspect of any movement is its beginning, giving the greatest credit to its pioneers. Another way to understand a movement is by giving credit to "baby steps" (my students' favorite phrase for every minute effort), assuming that each and every tiny step on the road to woman suffrage was equally vital. A third school of interpretation focuses on major turning points that pushed the movement forward at a particular time. Still other analyses stress underlying factors, big changes in society and economics that made progress possible. And, of course, within each interpretative framework historians may disagree about which pioneer, which small step, which factor, or which turning point was most decisive.

Even historians focusing on the 1917 victory rather than the early battles of the mid-nineteenth century differ in their interpretations. Goodier and Pastorello (2017) stress that the New York State victory required contributions from a wide variety of individuals and groups. Women in upstate rural New York, African American women, immigrants, and suffragist men, they believe, must be considered alongside the more famous white, middle- and upper-class activists in New York City. At the 2017 conference, describing what they consider a coalition of activists, Goodier depicted the movement as a "rich beautiful fabric that comes together that takes decades, and all kinds of people—black, white, Italian, Jewish, you name it." On the same panel, Lauren Santangelo argued that it was votes from the city, particularly from immigrant men, and most strongly Jewish socialist men, that made the difference in 1917.[3]

Happily, after decades without major scholarship on the final suffrage victory, the past few years have produced several intriguing, though differing, analyses. Johanna Neuman, author of *Gilded Age Suffragists: The New York Socialites who Fought for Women's Right to Vote*, gives credit to elite, stylish women who took suffrage from "frumpy to fashionable." Neuman (2015) reasons that such wealthy and influential women provided the first celebrity endorsement of a political campaign in the twentieth century, sparking renewed interest in the cause. In *Funding Feminism: Monied Women, Philanthropy, and the Women's Movement, 1870–1967*, Joan Marie Johnson (2017) stresses the importance of money to support all the apparatus (travel, publicity, staffing, communications) required by a modern movement. Brooke Kroeger's 2017 monograph *The Suffragents: How Women Used Men to Get the Vote* argues that the New York–based Men's League for Woman Suffrage played a vital role in the suffrage victory, both in New York State and nationally. Others, including Ann F. Lewis (2018), an experienced political strategist and major collector of suffrage memorabilia, insist that the New York leaders of NAWSA, particularly Carrie Chapman Catt and Mary Garrett Hay, deserve credit for the political campaign that delivered the vote. Some historians prefer to highlight the contributions of little-known figures like Maud Malone, "General" Rosalie Jones, Mabel Lee, Gertrude Bustill Mossell, and Sarah J. S. Tompkins Garnet, believing that credit for a movement that depended on diverse contributions must be shared among many (Meharg 2019; Jack 2016; Museum of the City of New York, n.d.). This position certainly has merit as a corrective to an exaggerated focus on leaders alone—but the press, politicians, and public hardly seem aware of Catt or other major suffrage leaders of 1917 (with the possible exception of Alice Paul). In classrooms and public talks, one rarely finds anyone who has ever even heard Catt's name.

The Argument for Carrie Chapman Catt

The debate over who deserves credit for the suffrage victories is not new. Even at the time of the suffrage victories in New York State (1917) and nationally (1920), suffragists themselves disagreed about who deserved recognition. Naturally, most felt that their own organization, tactics, and leaders were most responsible. For example, according to Neuman (2017, 141), Vira Boarman Whitehouse (president of the New York Suffrage Association from 1915 to 1917) "was widely credited with the win" and was hailed at the time as "the brilliant field-general of the New York State Suffrage army." Whitehouse was one of the wealthy socialites whose importance Neuman argues has been neglected in histories of the movement. Yet, as Neuman notes, Catt gave "no credit" (142) to Whitehouse in her own 1923 memoir, insisting instead that Mary Garrett Hay was responsible for the victory in New York City, which swung the state. Neuman suggests that it was her personal relationship with Hay that made Catt neglect Whitehouse's contributions (after Catt's return from Europe, she and Hay lived together as partners and are even buried together). But "Mollie" Hay did head the New York City Suffrage Party and was even known by reporters as "The Big Boss" (*New York Times* 1917b, 8; Perry 2019, 29).

Of course, this was a mass movement, and every individual's story is valuable. Yet to allow the name of Catt, the most prominent suffragist of the time—and leader of an organization (NAWSA) two million strong—to be forgotten, ignored, or even downplayed in our analysis seems counterproductive. If we are to learn from the ultimate success of this movement, we should look closely at its political campaigns, strategies, and tactics, as well as the individuals who developed and enacted them.

Catt's return to the United States in 1913 (from working for woman suffrage abroad) marked a turning point in both the New York State and the national movement. No eastern states allowed women to vote in state-wide or federal elections. In 1914, Miriam Leslie, a businesswoman and publisher, bequeathed to Catt a million dollars for the woman suffrage cause. Although the terms of the will were disputed, and Catt received only part of the original bequest, this infusion of funds greatly assisted the campaigns that followed (Johnson 2017, 39–40, 72–73).

1915: The Road to Victory Begins with Loss

The background to the 1917 New York State victory includes a heartbreaking 1915 loss in four eastern states: New York, Massachusetts, New Jersey, and Pennsylvania. The Empire State Campaign of 1913–1915 had been spearheaded by a unified committee with Catt as its chair, coordinating the efforts of the New York State Suffrage Association, the Woman Suffrage Party (WSP) in New York City with Hay as chair, and other groups. The Political Equality Association, headed by multimillionaire Alva Vanderbilt Belmont, and Harriot Stanton Blatch's Women's Political Union (an organization that focused on working women) organized separately.

Under Catt, the state was divided into twelve regional districts, 150 assembly districts, and 5,524 election districts, each with its own chair, leader, or captain.[4] According to Elisabeth Israels Perry (2019, 29), "the WSP under Hay's direction [in New York City] held 60 district conventions, 170 canvassing suppers, 4 mass meetings, 27 canvassing conferences, and a Carnegie Hall convention" and by Election Day, it had "held over 5,000 outdoor meetings, 660 indoor meetings, and 93 mass meetings." The campaign engaged both paid organizers and as many as two hundred thousand volunteers. Over ten thousand New York City public school teachers joined the Empire State Campaign, some giving up their summer vacations to "get down into the trenches" (Goodier and Pastorello 2017, 165).

According to suffragist Gertrude Foster Brown's retrospective analysis of 1940, the campaign was organized around the insight that

> it was useless to invite men to come to suffrage meetings. Where they were not opposed, they were indifferent, or considered the whole business a joke. Since they would not come to women, suffragists had to go to them wherever they were. (109)

An estimated seven million leaflets went out in twenty-four languages. Whitehouse chaired the publicity committee and raised money to fund its efforts. Stamps, posters, playing cards, pins, paper cups, and fans were produced and distributed around the state. Suffrage workers "approached letter carriers, conductors, motormen, subway workers, elevated guards, street sweepers, ticket sellers, firemen, and police" (Goodier and Pastorello 2017, 164). Hay "directed her followers to identify voters in every possible profession, craft, or job—from barbers to firemen, street cleaners to bankers, factory workers to clergy—and to create special days for each group" (Perry 2019, 29). Catt urged her volunteers to reach out to members of all religious affiliations, including Catholics and Jews. When Lyda D. Newman, an African American hairdresser and inventor, opened a suffrage headquarters in Manhattan, Hay sent representatives to coordinate activities with the WSP (Perry 2019, 29). Press and publicity departments not only spread the news of suffrage activities, but "undertook the task of creating news . . . and of seeing that anti-suffrage articles and editorials were adequately answered" (Brown 1940, 111). Meanwhile, Blatch and her independent Women's Political Union ran a separate campaign with its own speakers, meetings, and events (Cooney 2005, 269–71, 274–75, 282–83; Goodier and Pastorello 2017, 164–67).

The 1915 campaign culminated in a massive "Banner Parade" in New York City led by Catt and an international delegation of suffragists. More than a million spectators watched tens of thousands of women, who all wore white but marched amid a rainbow display of banners (Cooney 2005, 290–91; Lemak and Hopkins-Benton 2017, 152). Women "from every class and walk of life, and from every kind of employment were in line . . . all united for a common cause" (Brown 1940, 110). On the day of the vote, six thousand women were on hand as poll watchers, having been carefully prepared for this work by training schools (Perry 2019, 28; Brown 1940, 114).

Yet despite all the organizing, publicity, speeches, meetings, parades, rallies, and mementos distributed, regardless of the anticipation experienced by the suffragists themselves, woman suffrage was defeated in all four eastern states, even losing in New York City by more than 80,000 votes. Two nights after the defeat, Mary Garrett Hay chaired a meeting at Cooper Union to kick off a new campaign. The women immediately raised $100,000 in pledges and transformed the multiple organizations that had made up the Empire State Campaign into the New York State Woman Suffrage Party. Catt was chosen as its chair (Goodier and Pastorello 2017, 168.) Because suffragists aligned with Catt refused to accept defeat, the failed campaign of 1915 actually provided a strong starting point for the successful battle of 1917. In contrast, this loss caused Blatch to give up on the New York campaign, merge her organization (the Women's Political Union) with Alice Paul's Congressional Union, and focus solely on the federal amendment (Perry 2019, 30). Neither Blatch nor Paul was active in New York's 1917 drive, as both were working from Washington, DC.

1917: On to Victory

Although Catt had planned to head the 1917 New York campaign, she was unable to fulfill that role because the following month she was drafted to take the place of Anna Howard Shaw as president of NAWSA. At the emergency convention she called in September 1916, Catt revealed that NAWSA would now take the federal suffrage amendment as its major goal (previously, the group had put most of its effort into state-by-state campaigns like New York's, while Alice Paul's Congressional Union had favored a federal strategy). Catt's "Winning Plan" proposed that NAWSA focus simultaneously on state campaigns where success was likely and on a federal campaign, using state victories to influence and propel the eventual passage of a federal amendment. In 1916, NAWSA also convinced both the Republican and Democratic parties to include woman suffrage in their platforms.

With the advent of World War I in 1917, Catt set aside her lifelong pacifism and announced that NAWSA would work for a second goal: the war effort.[5] Catt had learned a lesson from Stanton and Anthony, who had put their push for women's rights on hold during the Civil War and subsequently regretted that decision. As she later wrote,

> the suffragists of 1917 had read history; they knew how prone men were to accept the help of suffragists in the hour of need and forget women's case for suffrage in the hour of calm. So while working loyally and energetically as special war organizations in support of the needs of the nation in its time of crisis, the New Yorkers did not lay aside their campaign. (Catt and Shuler 1923, 295)

1917: Effective Tactics

Though scholars may disagree about whom to credit for the ultimate suffrage victory, they all agree that new twentieth-century tactics making the struggle far more visible clearly made an important difference in the campaign. Flamboyant, popular events raised the profile of the movement and made it seem to be everywhere at once. With suffragists out in the streets of the cities and on the roadways of the state, they engaged in numerous spectacles in support of the vote. In 1913, for example, Long Island suffragist Edna Buckman Kearns used a wagon called "The Spirit of 1776" to attract attention and promote the cause, arguing against women's "taxation without representation."[6]

Lauren Santangelo (2017) points to the suffragists' use of urban space in general, and office buildings in particular, to enhance their prestige. As historian Jonathan Soffer (2012) has written of NAWSA,

> A board of wealthy women devoted themselves full time to the cause, creating a well-financed lobbying, advertising, and political organization. Headquartered on two floors of a Manhattan skyscraper, they deployed the latest technologies to persuade Americans of women's right to vote and maintained transnational and intercontinental connections. They transformed NAWSA into a modern, urban, cosmopolitan lobby for women's right to vote.

But how did this new visibility and publicity translate into an electoral victory? Ann F. Lewis argues that we need to examine the suffrage victory as a political campaign, not only as a social movement. The movement provided an underlying groundswell, but the campaign delivered the votes. Lewis asks, What did they *do* to win? Based on campaign literature and memorabilia (Lewis has collected over 1,200 items which are viewable online), her analysis considers their message, methods of persuasion, and the ability to turn out the vote (A. Lewis 2015). At the center of her analysis is the leadership of Carrie Chapman Catt and her longtime friend and companion Mary Garrett Hay (A. Lewis 2018).

In promoting the importance of Catt, Lewis focuses on such political moves as her 1914 address to the Federation of Women's Clubs, convincing this powerful group (long ambivalent about voting) that it was women's "duty" to fight for and use the ballot for good. Equally important was Hay's triumph in convincing Tammany Hall (the Democratic Party machine that controlled so many immigrant votes in New York City) to drop its opposition to the New York referendum. Her tactic was to appoint the wives of Tammany officers to positions of responsibility within the campaign.

Santangelo also recognizes the importance and innovation of Catt and NAWSA's contributions to the New York campaign by "mapping" the suffrage campaign's organization onto existing assembly districts. She argues that the suffragists came to see Manhattan as a "richly textured map" that could be understood as a collection of communities and neighborhoods. Goodier and Pastorello (2017) also give Catt appropriate credit, but their work sets her contributions in the context of a much larger movement as they strive to encompass decades of activism across the state.

1917: Why New York?

New York, the first state east of the Mississippi to support full suffrage for women, was targeted by suffrage leaders for two reasons: because the size of the New York delegation to Congress made it the most powerful addition to the suffrage cause and because it seemed most possible to pass a suffrage referendum in such a progressive state. That is, suffragists deliberately chose to focus on New York State as the most important, and the most likely, state to win in 1917.

The political process by which women suffragists attempted to win the vote was a referendum to amend the New York State Constitution. In order to get the referendum on the ballot, as they had in 1915, the measure had to be approved by two consecutive sessions of the state legislature. This meant that the referendum could be placed before the voters again quickly.

The presence of NAWSA's national headquarters in New York City and the position of Hay as chair of the Woman Suffrage Party in New York City also meant that significant political experience and focus were brought to bear on the city campaign. In addition, as described by Goodier and Pastorello in the preceding essay, New York had a strong state organization prepared to deliver votes across the state. In fact, women in the other eastern states where suffrage lost in 1915—New Jersey, Massachusetts, and Pennsylvania—did not win the vote until the federal amendment passed in 1920.

Suffragists were well aware of the pivotal position New York State could play in the national campaign. As the most populous state in the union, New York had the largest congressional delegation, whose representatives and senators would be forced to support a federal suffrage amendment once women could vote in the state. A victory in New York would begin to tip the scales and create what started to feel like inevitable momentum.

1917: The Right Moment

We know that the suffrage referendum failed in 1915 but passed in 1917, and that the difference in the vote came from New York City. According to Lauren Santangelo, who has studied the New York City campaign extensively, proposals from a constitutional convention held in 1915 disrupted the political landscape, leading suffragists to believe that men voted against their referendum when they went to vote against constitutional changes. In addition, Santangelo cites New York's polio epidemic of 1916 as an opportunity for Progressive women to prove their value as "municipal housekeepers." As volunteers passing out literature and assisting in inspections, women reformers demonstrated their skills and their willingness to cooperate with (for example, canceling their open-air meetings), assist, and support the government (Santangelo 2017).

Along with Goodier, Pastorello, and other scholars, I would also cite the immediate decision of Catt, Hay, and other suffrage leaders not to give up or even take time out after the 1915 defeat. Instead, they built on their previous efforts—essentially creating a four-year campaign that lasted from 1913 to 1917. To win in 1917, the movement also raised significantly more money. The state campaign of 1913–1915 started with a fund of less than $90,000; for the 1917 campaign, Whitehouse raised hundreds of thousands of dollars from wealthy men, and there was the extra infusion of cash from the Miriam Leslie bequest (Brown 1940, 117).

Suffragists continued to stress the importance of canvassing (soliciting votes or opinions one-on-one) in 1917. In order to prove that women *did* want the vote, and counter the anti-suffragists' argument that most women did not, they undertook a house-to-house canvas:

> To answer anti-suffragist charges that most women did not want to vote, suffragists spent more than a year going door-to-door in nearly every city and town in the state, collecting the signatures of over one million women who

said that they wanted to vote. Organizers climbed thousands of tenement stairs, walked country lanes, and visited the homes of the rich and poor. The result was the largest individually-signed petition ever assembled, eventually totaling 1,030,000 names, a majority of the women in the state. (Cooney 2005, 370)

To gain the vote in New York City (where the campaign had lost by more than eighty thousand votes in 1915), NAWSA organized an "effort focused on a combination of sophisticated advertising and block-by-block organizing, both particularly geared to the city's unrivalled population density and political culture" (Soffer 2012). Immigrant working-class heroines, like socialist labor organizer Rose Schneiderman, lobbied tirelessly to convince immigrant, working-class men to support suffrage for their mothers, wives, and daughters.

Finally, most scholars agree that the entry of the United States into World War I, and NAWSA's active support of the war effort, were important in turning the tide. Suffrage organizations also used the war to publicize their cause. For example, when distributing government pamphlets about conserving food or canning, suffragists were not shy about pasting on labels that promoted the suffrage referendum. In addition, suffragists lobbied soldiers and sailors at home and abroad, stressing women's support for the troops and courting their votes. Anti-suffragists, in contrast, supported the war wholeheartedly to the exclusion of their former campaigns.

On the eve of Election Day in 1917, Catt was quoted in the *New York Times* as appealing to the voters on the basis of the petition and American ideals:

Remember that our country is fighting for democracy, for the right of those who submit to authority to have a voice in their own government. Vote for woman suffrage, because it is part of the struggle toward democracy. (*New York Times* 1917c, 15)

In the end, suffrage won in every borough, and the large majority in the city overcame a slight loss upstate, so that the measure carried by more than a hundred thousand votes statewide. Suffrage won in

Auburn, Binghamton, Buffalo, Newburgh, Ossining, Oswego, Schenectady, Syracuse, and Westchester, but lost in Albany, Kingston, and Rochester (*New York Times* 1917a, 3). Hugely disappointed two years earlier, suffrage supporters were now jubilant.

On to 1920

In November 1917, as a result of multiple efforts and an army of volunteers, New York State passed the referendum supporting the vote for women in all elections. This put the power of the largest state in the union, with its congressional representatives, behind the Nineteenth Amendment. And, as the war continued, women's efforts—on the home front and overseas as drivers, nurses, telephone operators, and translators—increased, and were valued and praised. To do their part, women across the United States (not only suffragists) knit and nursed, but also worked in factories and on farms, filled in as office workers and streetcar conductors, drove ambulances, and even joined the navy as clerical workers. Women, whether or not active suffragists, proved their patriotism and citizenship. Meanwhile, NAWSA kept up its pressure on Congress and the president, as did Paul's National Woman's Party.

Women's leadership, organizational skills, and contributions of time, money, and energy led to the ultimate suffrage victory in 1920, when the Nineteenth Amendment to the US Constitution was finally ratified by the state of Tennessee, the thirty-sixth state to approve—thus meeting the required threshold for state support. The amendment passed by a single unexpected vote that was cast by a young representative from East Tennessee, Harry Burn. It seems that Burn's decision to vote in favor of the amendment was largely based on a letter he had received from his mother, Febb Ensminger Burn, who wrote that he should "be a good boy and help Mrs. Thomas [*sic*] Catt" (Burn 1920). Here is yet more evidence about the importance of Catt as the national leader of the suffrage campaign.

The suffrage victory called for celebration, and New York City was the site of a series of tributes to Catt. Her train was greeted at Penn Station by New York governor Al Smith (and a band), where Catt was almost overwhelmed by the huge bouquet given to her in tribute. An informal parade of suffrage workers then surrounded her car and marched to a reception at the Waldorf Astoria. Catt's arrival was met with thunderous applause.

Why Not Catt?

The lack of recognition of Catt as part of both the 1917 and 1920 centennials is shocking. Although women's historians may argue that she has been given too much credit, most Americans have never heard of her. While Susan B. Anthony's Rochester grave has become a site of pilgrimage, covered with "I Voted" stickers, the Woodlawn Cemetery monument for Catt and Hay receives little attention from the press or public—except from the LBGTQ community, who have on occasion placed pride flags next to the stone (Davis 2016). A recent children's book by Senator Kirsten Gillibrand, *Bold and Brave: Ten Heroes Who Won Women the Right to Vote*, does not even include Catt as one of the ten leaders, though it features other women who were not very active in the suffrage movement. Almost unbelievably, "Votes for Women" (2019), a five-hundred-piece puzzle and matching set of informational flash cards portraying forty-one US suffragists, also ignores Catt (in favor, it appears, of mixing iconic figures such as Stanton, Anthony, Truth, Mott, Paul, and Frederick Douglass with a wide range of relative unknowns who provide both geographic and racial diversity).

During Catt's lifetime, everyone knew her name and the press gave her credit for the suffrage victory. In 1912, her picture appeared on a full-page spread in the Sunday *New York Times*, featuring her international suffrage campaign; in 1926, Catt appeared on the cover of *Time* magazine (*New York Times* 1912, SM8; *Time* 1926). When she died in 1947, Catt's obituary in the *New York Times* stated categorically that "when the Nineteenth Amendment was ratified, she was the national heroine of a great victory. More than anyone else, she had turned Woman Suffrage from a dream into a fact . . . Her attack was logical, organized, and unanswerable" (*New York Times* 1947, 20).

Why has Catt been written out of the popular suffrage story? Her racism and anti-immigrant attitudes could be blamed, but here she was certainly no different from—no worse than—Anthony, Stanton, or Paul. We can assume that like most Americans, white, middle-class suffrage leaders were all racists to some extent, particularly if they were from the South. Certainly, the evidence shows that both Catt and Alice Paul were willing to accommodate racism in order to pass the federal suffrage amendment. Famously, Paul told African American women to march as a segregated unit, at the back of the line, in her great Washington, DC, suffrage parade of 1913. Although African American leader Mary Church Terrell claimed that Catt (whom she considered a friend) showed no signs of personal racism, Catt made no effort to advocate for racial equality, or even allow issues of racial justice to be discussed at NAWSA conventions (Wagner 2019, 486).

Ann F. Lewis suggests that Catt's lack of recognition could be because neither she nor her tactics make a good picture. Suffragists may have gone from "frumpy to fashionable" as Neuman (2015) argues, but Catt and Hay remained distinctly frumpy. Alice Paul and Lucy Burns (both included in Gillibrand's children's book) were young and photogenic, but by the time of the suffrage victory, Catt was in her late 50s and early 60s, with dark circles ringing her eyes, and dressed in shapeless cloaks and gowns. While the demonstrators of the National Women's Party could be pictured picketing the White House, being arrested, or even sitting in jail, the lobbying and strategizing sessions led by Catt just do not make for good visuals.

There are geographic issues as well. Seneca Falls and Rochester, in the western part of New York State, have actively promoted their suffrage sites to encourage tourism. New York City, where Catt and Hay organized their campaigns, and Westchester, where they lived, have numerous attractions but little has been done to make a suffrage trail through these areas.

Perhaps most important is the fact that Catt was moderate and accommodationist, an organizer and a politician. Her "Winning Plan" of 1916 won the vote in only four years. But it seems that many feminists don't want her to have been responsible. Today's activists prefer someone more confrontational, more radical—someone more like Susan B. Anthony, who was tried for voting illegally, or Alice Paul, who insulted President Wilson in the midst of World War I. However, our presentism should not blind us to the complex realities of the past. Flawed as she was, Catt must be recognized as a successful leader. She was a consummate political organizer; she accepted that getting the win required compromises and mixed tactics, as well as different approaches for different populations of voters. Neither "great men" nor "great women" should have to be perfect to be remembered.[7]

Where Are We Now?

In conclusion, disagreements among suffrage scholars, as discussed above, are a very positive sign of the vitality of recent research into the 1917 and 1920 suffrage victories. Like all other important historical events in US history, the long struggle to end voting discrimination on the basis of sex deserves a robust historiography, including passionate debates. Historians are ready to move beyond Susan B. Anthony and other nineteenth-century heroines, and to analyze the successful suffrage campaigns of the early twentieth century. The wealth of recent publications provides a substantial reading list for anyone inspired to learn more about the movement. In addition to all the titles previously mentioned and cited, important new studies published in 2019 include Susan Ware's *Why They Marched: The Untold Stories of the Women Who Fought for the Right to Vote*, Sally Roesch Wagner's *The Women's Suffrage Movement*, and Santangelo's *Suffrage and the City: New York Women Battle for the Ballot*. Elaine Weiss's *The Women's Hour: The Great Fight to Win the Vote* is even (according to the cover) "soon to be a major television event." Forthcoming volumes include Neuman's *And Yet They Persisted: How American Women Won the Right to Vote*.

Research into this important topic is ongoing, while public appreciation of the complexity of issues surrounding the suffrage victory is only beginning. We trust that the centennial celebrations of 2017 have provided the spark to open up a vast new area of inquiry for 2020 and beyond. As Ann F. Lewis points out, the passage of the Nineteenth Amendment represented the greatest expansion of suffrage in this nation's history. Surely it is time that the multiple stories surrounding the final campaign—especially the leadership of Carrie Chapman Catt—become well known to the public and students across the United States. Finally, it is vital that feminists analyze the successful tactics and strategies of the past to see if they can prove useful in addressing the limits of suffrage today.

Notes

1. The idea for this essay grew out of two stimulating discussions at our 2017 "Women in Politics" conference commemorating the centennial of the suffrage victory in New York State. The first was a keynote conversation between Eleanor Roosevelt scholar Allida Black and political strategist Ann F. Lewis, which took place at the Franklin D. Roosevelt Presidential Library on the first evening of the program. The second was a panel featuring three suffrage historians—Susan Goodier, Karen Pastorello, and Lauren Santangelo—with me as moderator, which took place the following morning at SUNY New Paltz. My interpretation has also been informed by teaching two courses on the suffrage movement in the academic year 2016–2017, especially the research and analysis of my students, including posters they presented at the conference. My own interest in this topic began with a blog entry, "Women Win the Right to Vote in New York State," posted on *New York Rediscovered* in November 2013 (https://sites.newpaltz.edu/nyrediscovered/2013/11/06/women-win-the-right-to-vote-in-new-york-state/). The following summer, I had the opportunity to collaborate with Professor Laura Dull and three former students—Sarah Sebald, Matt Grande, and Alyson Dodge—on a women's rights curriculum adaptable for upper elementary, middle school, high school, and college students: *Women's Rights: The Struggle Continues*, freely available online (https://www.newpaltz.edu/schoolofed/cie/womenrights.html). As part of the 2017 conference, these alumni, now teachers, presented their unit plans during a continuing education workshop facilitated by Robin Jacobowitz entitled "Incorporating Women's Political History into the K–12 Curriculum."

2. For example, the Humanities New York reading list "Votes for Women!" included a volume on Seneca Falls (published in 2009), a biography of Stanton (2010), a biography of Alice Paul (2010), a book on African American women and the vote (1998), a historical novel set in Gilded Age New York (2005), and a collection of essays (2002), many of which dealt with the nineteenth century. This collection did include a thirteen-page chapter on Carrie Chapman Catt, though balanced by a fifteen-page chapter on Paul. See https://humanitiesny.org/our-work/programs/reading-discussion/votes-for-women/.

3. Here Santangelo is citing Elinor Lerner's 1981 dissertation, "Immigrant and Working Class Involvement in the New York City Woman Suffrage Movement, 1905–1917: A Study in Progressive Era Politics."

4. Detailed descriptions of the 1915 and 1917 campaigns appear in Gertrude Foster Brown's "A Decisive Victory Is Won," Chapter 9 of the National American Woman Suffrage Association's *Victory, How Women Won It* (1940); Chapter 1, "Precedents," in Perry's *After the Vote* (2019); Chapter

15, "Winning New York," in Cooney's *Winning the Vote* (2005); and Chapter 9, "Rising from the Ashes of Defeat," in Goodier and Pastorello's *Women Will Vote* (2017).

5. After the war, Catt devoted much of her activism to the cause of world peace.

6. Buckman's granddaughter, Marguerite Kearns, has tirelessly promoted the story of this wagon and lobbied to have it permanently displayed at the New York State Museum in Albany. It was on display in the museum lobby as part of the *Votes for Women: Celebrating New York's Suffrage Centennial* exhibit from November 4, 2017 to May 13, 2018. See http://www.suffragewagon.org/about-the-spirit-of-1776-wagon/.

7. In fact, one might argue that our current political climate (all or nothing) and our current painful gridlock is a direct result of the refusal to compromise and do the actual work of governing.

Works Cited

Brown, Gertrude Foster. 1940. "A Decisive Victory Won." In *Victory, How Women Won It: A Centennial Symposium, 1840–1940*, edited by the National American Woman Suffrage Association, 105–20. New York: H. H. Wilson.

Burn, Phoebe Ensminger. 1920. Letter to Harry Burn. Harry T. Burn Papers. Knox County Public Library, Knoxville, TN. http://cmdc.knoxlib.org/cdm/ref/collection/p265301coll8/id/699.

Catt, Carrie Chapman, and Nettie Rogers Shuler. 1923. *Woman Suffrage and Politics: The Inner Story of the Suffrage Movement*. Seattle: University of Washington Press.

Cooney, Robert P. J., Jr. 2005. *Winning the Vote: The Triumph of the American Woman Suffrage Movement*. Half Moon Bay, CA: American Graphic Press.

———. 2012. "How New York Women Won Equal Suffrage 100 Years Ago." National Women's History Project. NWHP Blog. August 2, 2012. http://www.americangraphicpress.com/articlesphotographs.html.

Davis, Amanda. 2016. "Placing Pride Flags at Woodlawn Cemetery." NYC LGBT Historic Sites Project. June 2, 2016. https://www.nyclgbtsites.org/2016/06/02/placing-pride-flags-at-woodlawn-cemetery/.

Fowler, Robert Booth. 1986. *Carrie Catt: Feminist Politician*. Boston: Northeastern University Press.

Goodier, Susan. 2013. *No Votes for Women: The New York State Anti-suffrage Movement*. Urbana: University of Illinois Press.

Goodier, Susan, and Karen Pastorello. 2017. *Women Will Vote: Winning Suffrage in New York State*. Ithaca, NY: Cornell University Press.

Jack, Zachary M. 2016. *March of the Suffragettes: Rosalie Gardiner Jones and the March for Voting Rights*. San Francisco, CA: Zest Books.

Johnson, Joan Marie. 2017. *Funding Feminism: Monied Women, Philanthropy, and the Women's Movement, 1870–1967*. Chapel Hill: University of North Carolina Press.

Kroeger, Brooke. 2017. *The Suffragents: How Women Used Men to Get the Vote*. Albany: State University of New York Press.

Lemak, Jennifer A., and Ashley Hopkins-Benton. 2017. *Votes for Women: Celebrating New York's Suffrage Centennial*. Albany: State University of New York Press.

Lerner, Elinor. 1981. "Immigrant and Working Class Involvement in the New York City Woman Suffrage Movement, 1905–1917: A Study in Progressive Era Politics." PhD diss., University of California, Berkeley.

Lewis, Ann F. 2015. Ann Lewis Women's Suffrage Collection. Updated May 2015. https://lewissuffragecollection.omeka.net/.

———. 2018. "Messaging, Media, and Motherhood: Political Strategies of the New York Suffrage Campaign." Speech at New York State Museum, April 15, 2018.

Lewis, Susan Ingalls. 2013. "Women Win the Right to Vote in New York State." *New York Rediscovered* (blog), November 6, 2013. https://sites.newpaltz.edu/nyrediscovered/2013/11/06/women-win-the-right-to-vote-in-new-york-state/.

Meharg, Dan. 2019. "Maude Malone: Suffrage Pioneer." National Park Service. Last modified July 5, 2019. https://www.nps.gov/articles/maud-malone-suffrage-pioneer.htm.

Museum of the City of New York. n.d. "Beyond Suffrage: 'Working Together, Working Apart' How Identity Shaped Suffragists' Politics." Accessed November 11, 2019. https://www.mcny.org/lesson-plans/beyond-suffrage-working-together-working-apart-how-identity-shaped-suffragists.

Neuman, Johanna. 2017. *Gilded Suffragists: The New York Socialites Who Fought for Women's Right to Vote*. New York: New York University Press.

New York Times. 1912. "Mrs. Catt Crusading around the World for Suffrage." June 23, 1912.

New York Times. 1917a. "Suffrage Made Gains Up-state." November 7, 1917.

New York Times. 1917b. "Suffragists' Machine Perfected in All States under Mrs. Catt's Rule." April 29, 1917.

New York Times. 1917c. "Suffragists Make Final State Appeal: Great Promise of Victory in New York, Says Mrs. Carrie Chapman Catt." November 5, 1917.

New York Times. 1947. "Carrie Chapman Catt." March 10, 1947.

Patterson, Martha. 2005. *Beyond the Gibson Girl: Reimagining the American New Woman, 1895–1915*. Champaign: University of Illinois Press.

————. 2008. *The American New Woman Revisited: A Reader*. New Brunswick, NJ: Rutgers University Press.

Perry, Elizabeth Israels. 2019. *After the Vote: Feminist Politics in La Guardia's New York*. Oxford: Oxford University Press.

Santangelo, Lauren. 2017. "1917: How Did Women Win the Vote in New York State?" Panel discussion at Women in Politics, Past, Present & Future: A Conference Commemorating the Centennial of Women's Suffrage in New York State, State University of New York at New Paltz, April 23, 2017. http://www.newpaltz.edu/benjamincenter/events/women-in-politics-past-present--future/.

Santangelo, Lauren. 2019. *Suffrage and the City: New York Women Battle for the Ballot*. New York: Oxford University Press.

Soffer, Jonathan. 2012. "Modern Women Persuading Modern Men: The Nineteenth Amendment and the Movement for Woman Suffrage, 1916–1920." *History Now*, no. 30 (Winter 2012). Gilder Lehrman Institute of American History. https://www.gilderlehrman.org/history-now/modern-women-persuading-modern-men-nineteenth-amendment-and-movement-woman-suffrage-1916.

Time. 1926. (Cover.) June 14, 1926.

Van Voris, Jacqueline. 1987. *Carrie Chapman Catt: A Public Life*. New York: Feminist Press.

Wagner, Sally Roesch. 2019. *The Women's Suffrage Movement*. New York: Penguin Books.

Ware, Susan. 2019. *Why They Marched: The Untold Stories of the Women Who Fought for the Right to Vote*. Cambridge, MA: Belknap Press of Harvard University Press.

Weiss, Elaine. 2019. *The Woman's Hour: The Great Fight to Win the Vote*. New York: Penguin Books.

Chapter 3

After the Vote

Continuing the Struggle for Women's Social, Legal, and Political Equality

JULIE A. GALLAGHER, JOANNA L. GROSSMAN,
AND MEG DEVLIN O'SULLIVAN

New York suffragists, as well as those advocating for a federal constitutional amendment, labored under the expectation that women would achieve greater gender parity and full rights of citizenship once they attained the vote. However, the post-suffrage trajectory of women's equality in New York State and the United States establishes that the path to women's equality would not accord with such logic. First, the narrative that all women gained the franchise in 1920 defies the historic reality. Although New York State was not beset by the state-sanctioned white supremacy of the Jim Crow South—which rendered voting a near impossibility for black women—Native American women who held citizenship in their indigenous nations would not officially earn federal voting rights until the 1924 Indian Citizenship Act. Second, as this chapter argues, the right to vote did not result in immediate structural economic, political, and cultural change for women or American society more generally. As the post-suffrage political struggles of women make clear, the franchise, while crucial for participation in a representative democracy, was a limited tool. Thus, women marshaled other strategies to effect political change.

This chapter toggles between the macro view of national trends that speak to limited advances in equality that woman suffrage yielded and the New York story that tracks the efforts of a number of politically active African American women—some of the most historically marginalized members of a society that predicated political power on white masculinity. In so doing, this essay illuminates important turning points and hard-won victories as well as limitations and preservations of the status quo. Over twenty years ago, Nancy Cott argued for the continuity of women's political work in her assessment of the decades that surround suffrage (Cott 1995, 353–73). Such a framework applies to the analyses advanced here. Conceiving of suffrage as an important political moment—but not a cultural watershed—clarifies the continuous nature of the larger struggle for justice. Moreover, the political experiences that women had before, beyond, and beside the right to vote instructed them in their post-suffrage efforts. Politically engaged black women in New York offer an instructive case study to analyze the strategic ways women endeavored to advance their goals through state-centered activism after they won the right to vote. While national trends speak to a decidedly limited set of gains for women that resulted from the franchise, a view of the state and local levels enables us to glean the slivers of opportunity that women were able to create and seize, thus translating political rights into social and cultural change.

In 1915, in anticipation of the statewide constitutional vote in New York, women took to the streets, argued on the pages of local newspapers, paraded down Gotham's wide avenues, and courageously faced off against those who believed that the most fundamental expression of citizenship should remain exclusively in men's hands (*New York Times*, May 6, 1911, 12; May 5, 1912, 1; *Crisis* 1915; DuBois 1997). Some women made the case for women's right to the franchise based on reason: "By what logic can you argue that her equality is not of man's? . . . I urge that women in politics is a necessity," proclaimed Helen Holman, a popular and fervent Harlem-based political activist (*New York Age* April 22, 1915, 5). Holman justified women's right to vote based not only on the substantial contributions women made in the workplace, the home, and society, but also on the merits of racial justice. Holman, an outspoken activist, urged that "we must enter politics to rear our race with health" (*Philadelphia Tribune* 1916, 3).

New Yorkers voted down the amendment in 1915, but determined suffragists made sure it was on the ballot again two years later. By early November 1917, New York City convulsed with excitement over the upcoming vote. Suffragists finally broke through the thick walls of resistance, particularly in New York City, home of the infamous Democratic Party political machine Tammany Hall, and in so doing more than one million New York women gained the right to vote.

After they secured the vote, most New York women did not expect the political process to transform the injustices of society immediately or completely. Nevertheless, they sought to make the state responsive to their demands (Skowronek 1982, ix, 285; Clemens 1999, 91). In particular, black women understood that if they were not at the table raising concerns that affected their lives and those in African American communities across the state, no one would. While they held diverse political beliefs, they tended to be more pragmatic than ideological in their struggles for improved housing, schools, jobs, and health care, as well as political participation. Like women across the nation, black women embraced the ballot, but they also ventured into political clubhouses, initiated legal cases, petitioned legislators, and ran for office. These women evinced ideas about the expansive role government could play in creating a more just society and they, like many women across the country, fought to bring that about.

At the same time, nationally, in the years surrounding the adoption of the Nineteenth Amendment, legal and political commentators vigorously debated the rights and duties incidental to voting.[1] Women's rights advocates relied on formal citizenship status as a basis for demanding the substantive rights that full citizens enjoy—a broad spectrum of political, personal, and civil rights from suffrage to child custody to property ownership. Many women had been fighting for these rights for decades, most of which were predicated on the 1848 Seneca Falls Convention's Declaration of Sentiments, a wish list that would serve as the blueprint for a century of women's rights advocacy.[2] The civil and political rights emphasized by those early advocates were essential components of equal citizenship, a substantive concept codified and popularized roughly one hundred years later by British social theorist T. H. Marshall. "Citizenship," Marshall (1964, 84) wrote, "is a status bestowed on those who are full members of a community. All who possess the status are equal with respect to the rights and duties with which the status is endowed."

Between the legal Jim Crow structures in the South and the culture of Jim Crow in the North, African Americans in New York had a deep appreciation of the gap between the promise of equality that the category of citizenship suggested and the very real, and at times deadly, practices of discrimination. They understood that the promise that the Fifteenth Amendment had held for black men's full rights of citizenship, quickly broken during and after Reconstruction, was similarly fraught in regard to the expansion of the franchise to women. Still, with limited options with which to fight racial and gender inequality, African American women ventured forth.

Nationally, hopes that the right to vote would be an indicator of full citizenship were quickly dashed. Courts routinely held that suffrage was just suffrage and did not serve as a gateway to other civil or political rights long denied to women.[3] As Reva Siegel (2002, 1012) has argued, "Soon after ratification, the judiciary moved to repress the structural significance of women's enfranchisement, by reading the Nineteenth Amendment as a rule concerning voting that had no normative significance for matters other than the franchise." Even with such limitations, African American women in New York, like Holman, recognized that they now had a tool their sisters in the Jim Crow South did not, and they were determined to use it. Voter education campaigns proliferated. The New York Times ran a series titled "The Woman Voter" and the New York Age noted that "colored women . . . are talking politics with zest and enthusiasm" (New York Times, January 6, 1918, 18; January 7, 1918, 14; January 8, 1918, 16; New York Age, November 22, 1917, 1). On the eve of the first presidential election after the Nineteenth Amendment's ratification, the editors of the New York Age urged women to "get the practice of marking a ballot." At the same time, their lingering doubt about women's fitness to handle the franchise seeped through as the editors encouraged women to "permit men to assist them in it" (New York Age, September 18, 1920, 4). In their pursuit of political power, black women in New York City contended with racism and sexism and the effects of their intersectional dynamics long after they secured the franchise. Nevertheless, motivated primarily by the desire to redirect economic, social, and political resources through the government to the black communities they lived in, and to undo the system of racial inequality at all levels, they worked to get political parties to take them seriously as constituents, candidates, and eventually as elected officials.

Leaders in the Democratic and Republican parties strategized ways to benefit from the new constituents flooding the voter rolls.

Both parties fielded a handful of white women for state assembly seats immediately after the suffrage amendment passed, and as a result the first women claimed their place in the statehouse. The Republican Party went further than the Democrats in its outreach to black women and selected a few African American women to represent their districts at the state and national party conventions. These modest gestures revealed that women were not only eager to participate in party politics but, if given a chance, perhaps they could win. For black women who wanted to run for office, however, the intersectional dynamics of racism and sexism kept them off the political parties' radar screens almost completely.

National conditions corresponded with some of the challenges black women faced in New York. Broadly speaking, women gained little in terms of rights or status in the first four decades after suffrage was won. Politically as well as civilly, they remained second-class citizens and, when they challenged particular types of disadvantage and discrimination, found as little redress from the judiciary as they did from electoral politics, although there were exceptional moments. In 1919, two years after women won the right to vote in New York, for example, Coral Smith was hired as a nurse at Bellevue Hospital in Manhattan and then fired two days later because "colored nurses were not employed at that institution" (*New York Age*, November 1, 1919, 1). She brought a legal suit against the hospital, charging that her dismissal was a violation of New York State's Civil Rights Law. Although Smith's struggle to break down the Jim Crow door took over a year, by May 1921, the hospital revised its practices because of further prodding by Harlem alderman Charles Roberts, one of two African American legislators at the time. The hospital promised to hire African American nurses from that point forward.[4] To the extent that black women's votes buttressed African American men in city government, the law in this case was compelled to support the women. Such was not the case for Natalie Stewart, however, who despite passing civil service exams with top grades, was repeatedly passed over for jobs she was eminently qualified for. The Civil Service Commission refused to address the problem, arguing that it was "powerless to prevent discrimination" by city and state institutions (*New York Age* April 30, 1927, 1).

Although there were minor victories like Smith's, Stewart's situation reflected the national trends women faced for decades after the vote. In 1948, for example, the United States Supreme Court upheld a Michigan law that prohibited female bartenders unless the bar was owned by a woman's husband or father (*Goesaert v. Cleary* 1948). As late as 1961, the Supreme Court upheld Florida's juror registration system, which granted automatic exemptions to women based on stereotyped assumptions about their family responsibilities and availability for service (*Hoyt v. Florida* 1961). These rulings from the 1920s through the 1960s reflected the widely held belief that men and women were different and were not entitled to equal treatment in civil or political life, which rendered women's participation in electoral politics even more necessary.

Woman suffrage did little to undermine the deeply entrenched association of masculinity with public citizenship, in the courts and at the ballot box. Not a single woman was elected to the New York State legislature between 1920 and 1933. But by the early 1930s, small fractures began to appear in the walls of resistance to women in electoral politics. The prominence of women in community activism, many with roots in the Progressive Era; the unprecedented national economic crisis; and the increased numbers of women on voter reg- istration rolls led a number of black women, including Layle Lane, Eunice Carter, Jane Bolin, Ruth Whitehead Whaley, and Sara Pelham Speaks, to run for elected office in New York City during the 1930s. Each hoped to gain access to the fruits of political power to help their struggling communities.

To illustrate, Layle Lane's efforts suggest both the determination and the challenges women faced. A teacher by profession, Lane was a fierce civil rights activist, a committed labor leader, and an ardent socialist who believed deeply in the centrality of the state to the alle- viation of poverty and racial discrimination. Convinced that grassroots efforts alone would not solve the problems African Americans in New York faced with discrimination in housing, jobs, and education, Lane turned to politics. Throughout her 1934 campaign for the US Congress, she argued that the government needed to aggressively step in to address injustices. As with many other leftists, she also favored price controls and government-supported full employment programs. Ultimately, Lane went down in defeat, but she was hardly deterred. She ran for office eight more times and remained committed to the idea that elected office could help bring about "economic security for all" (Lane 1941, 10). Throughout the 1930s and 1940s, Lane was one of over a dozen African American women who found increasing support among the GOP, the Socialist Party, the American Labor Party (formed in 1936), and the Liberal Party (formed in 1944). But in a city dominated by the Democratic Party, politically ambitious African American women ran into a wall of obstinacy. Active in the party, black women worked to chip away at Tammany Hall's resistance. But when and how would change finally come to New York City and State?

By 1954, Bessie Buchanan, a loyal Democrat, was well known in the Harlem community. A former dancer and screen star, she was a close friend of Josephine Baker's.[5] Just as importantly, Buchanan had proven herself to the Tammany leadership. That year, she seized an opportunity created by a struggle within Tammany's ranks to make her bid for office for the state assembly. Black women outnumbered black men on voter registration lists and Buchanan actively courted them.[6] Her campaign platform included something for African Americans in general and something for black women in particular. She pledged to fight for "stronger anti-discrimination laws, more day care centers and increased unemployment and workmen's compensation benefits," demonstrating a concern for race, gender, and class issues (*Amsterdam News*, October 23, 1954, 2). Buchanan's local popularity, the Democratic Party's support, the record number of women on voter registration rolls, and the trend for African Americans to vote Democratic all worked in her favor. She soundly defeated her opponent and made history as the first black woman elected to office in New York. She headed to Albany, where she made good on her promise to fight against all forms of discrimination (*Amsterdam News*, November 6, 1954, 1; *New York Times*, November 4, 1954, 27; *New York State Legislative Record and Index*). The first bills Buchanan introduced addressed pay inequities based on sex, as well as racial discrimination in banking, education, and insurance. She teamed up with a few liberal colleagues and reintroduced these and other civil rights bills every year but made no progress getting them translated into law. Nevertheless, she helped bring a new level of attention to both women's issues and civil rights issues.[7] These efforts also helped build momentum for important changes that transpired in the 1960s.

Nationally and in New York, the tides began to turn with the renewed energy of the women's movement in the 1960s and 1970s. Responding to a variety of social, economic, and political movements, women's rights advocates litigated, lobbied, and spoke out against the many ways in which women were disadvantaged in American society relative to men. Discrimination and social injustices in jobs, housing, education, and politics—problems that women had been fighting for the past four decades—were now raised before leaders of the liberal political establishment at the national level. Invited for the first time to participate in these national conversations were a number of African American women who had forged their political skills in New York City over the previous four decades. These included Dorothy Height, president of the National Council of Negro Women (NCNW), and Pauli Murray, a legal activist. Both made significant contributions to the President's Commission on the Status of Women (PCSW) meetings as well as the policy recommendations that resulted from them, including the Equal Pay Act of 1963. During the same period, Murray also offered a powerful defense for including the issue of sex discrimination in Title VII of the 1964 Civil Rights Act (Murray and Eastwood 1965, 233; Murray 1964, 9).

Beginning in 1971, the Supreme Court recognized that sex-based classifications in state and federal laws were very likely to reflect the stereotypes and assumptions about women that had led to their inferior treatment by the government throughout history. The court held that lower courts must subject sex-based classifications challenged under the Equal Protection Clause to heightened scrutiny, a standard that required the government to prove it was pursuing an important governmental interest to which the sex-based classification was substantially related (*Reed v. Reed* 1971). Under this exacting standard, state and federal codes were slowly purged of the sex-based distinctions and rules that pervaded them. For instance, Congress had to stop presuming that servicemen had dependent wives but servicewomen had breadwinning husbands (*Frontiero v. Richardson* 1973). Similar legal decisions were handed down around the country. Alabama had to eliminate the rule that only men could be forced to pay alimony after divorce (*Orr v. Orr* 1979). Oklahoma had to stop allowing girls to buy beer at a younger age than boys (thus changing a law that seemingly privileged young girls by facilitating their access to alcohol) (*Craig v. Boren* 1976). Elimination of these distinctions was necessary to level the playing field for women—to allow them to stand as equals with men in society. As Justice Ruth Bader Ginsburg later wrote in her majority opinion in *United States v. Virginia* (1996), in which the court struck down the male-only admissions policy of the Virginia Military Institute,

"Neither federal nor state government acts compatibly with equal protection when a law or official policy denies to women, simply because they are women, full citizenship stature—equal opportunity to aspire, achieve, participate in and contribute to society based on their individual talents and capacities."

Simultaneously, the 1960s and 1970s brought further breakthroughs that linked New York State politics to the national stage. Shirley Chisholm, a Brooklyn native and member of the New York State Assembly, became the first black woman elected to Congress in 1968. Schooled in Brooklyn's Democratic Party clubhouses as well as an insurgent organization, the United Democratic Club, Chisholm was a savvy politician. She scored her first political victory in 1964, handily winning a seat in the state assembly. Four years later, with the enthusiastic support of her female-dominated constituency, Chisholm decisively defeated the formidable civil rights activist James Farmer for the newly created Twelfth Congressional District seat in Brooklyn. Once in Washington, Chisholm put the needs of African Americans, women, and the poor at the center of her legislative program, cosponsoring bills that proposed educational opportunities for those who needed it, health insurance for domestic workers, federal funding increases for housing, welfare reforms that substantively supported impoverished women without punishment or judgment, the passage of the Equal Rights Amendment, and the repeal of laws that made abortion illegal (*Congressional Record* 1969). Her vision was bold and activist; her capacity to shepherd it through Congress proved to be another matter. Without well-placed senior legislators who would support her legislative agenda, and with small cohorts of white women and African American men in Congress, Chisholm and other women legislators found the congressional arena a difficult one in which to effect change.

Yet they did score some important legislative victories, which were necessary components of women's workplace equality. Spearheaded by women who worked from inside the halls of Congress—despite the discrimination they faced—and simultaneously pushed by grassroots activists and women's organizations outside, Congress passed the Equal Pay Act of 1963. The PCSW required employers to pay women the same as men for doing equal work for the same employer (29 USC § 206(d) [2012]). Title VII of the Civil Rights Act of 1964, which Pauli Murray so eloquently defended in a memo to the wavering

Senate, prohibited discrimination based on a variety of identity traits, including sex (42 USC § 2000e-17 [2012]). These two cornerstone laws were supplemented in later years by the important protections of Title IX of the Education Amendments of 1972, which prohibits sex discrimination by educational institutions receiving any federal financial assistance. This vital piece of legislation resulted from the strategic advocacy of women in Congress, including Patsy Mink, the first Asian American woman elected to Congress; Shirley Chisholm; and veteran politician Edith Green. The Pregnancy Discrimination Act of 1978, which amends Title VII of the Civil Rights Act to prohibit discrimination also because of "pregnancy, childbirth, or related medical conditions," was also the result of concerted efforts by women in Congress, including Mink and Chisholm. And the importance of having women in Congress could be seen in the Family and Medical Leave Act of 1993, which guarantees employees of larger companies the right to twelve weeks of unpaid leave per year as needed for pregnancy-related disability, childbirth, or new parenting (Title IX 1972; Pregnancy Discrimination Act 1978; Family and Medical Leave Act 2012).

Although the discrimination laws were an essential step in establishing women's workplace and educational equality, the courts played a crucial role in establishing understandings of discrimination against women and the guiding principles that shaped the equality landscape. For example, in a 1986 case, the Supreme Court held that sexual harassment is a form of intentional sex discrimination and is actionable under Title VII (Meritor Sav. Bank v. Vinson 1986). The court also recognized that discrimination against a subset of women— for example, a company's refusal to hire women with preschool-age children—is as illegal as discrimination against all women (Phillips v. Martin Marietta Corp. 1971). And perhaps most importantly, the court held that Title VII prohibits decisions motivated by sex-role stereotyping; for instance, a woman cannot legally be fired for being insufficiently feminine (Price Waterhouse v. Hopkins 1989). Together, these statutes and judicial opinions erected a regime in which public and private entities could neither continue to exclude women with impunity nor demand that they live up to stereotypical roles once admitted to the institutions of civil society. Equally crucial to women's economic empowerment was the recognition of a constitutional right of privacy that gave women greater control over the number and timing of pregnancies through the right of access to contraception, the right to terminate a pregnancy before a certain point, and the right not to be excluded from workplace opportunities on the basis of reproductive capacity.[8] As the Supreme Court observed in its 1992 abortion rights ruling in *Planned Parenthood v. Casey*, the "ability of women to participate equally in the economic and social life of the Nation has been facilitated by their ability to control their reproductive lives."

Conclusion

In New York State, feminists from the 1910s to the 1970s contributed enormously to women's equality by breaking down barriers to participation in political life and the workplace, among other places. But one would be remiss to conclude that the fight for women's equality is over. Although women now compose about half of the American labor force, their experiences are anything but equal.[9] Women continue to get paid less than men for doing the same work, and women of color still lag far behind white women in terms of wages and job opportunities. Women experience sexual harassment at surprisingly high rates—which became even more apparent with the emergence of the #MeToo movement—and suffer employment consequences when they complain. The United States ranks last among industrialized countries in the provision of paid leave and other support for working parents. The labor force in every sector of the economy resembles a pyramid in that women's representation starts strong at the bottom and then decreases, often substantially, with every move up the ladder. Jobs remain highly segregated by gender, and women who attempt to infiltrate traditionally male-dominated jobs encounter relentless hostility. Women continue to perform the bulk of child-rearing tasks, even when they work the same hours as their male partners. Pregnancy and motherhood still seem to befuddle employers, and the law has been slow to provide accommodations that would make it easier for women to maintain workforce attachments through the demanding years of childbearing. Women, especially women of color, continue to be disadvantaged by both explicit and implicit bias that seem impervious to change. Women face challenges outside the workplace as well, ranging from domestic violence to disproportionate rates of poverty to inaccessible healthcare.

This gap between the promise of equal citizenship that was expected from the franchise and the persistence of discrimination describes much of the post-suffrage world for US women. It was especially salient for African American women who contended with racism and sexism and the effects of their intersectional dynamics. Nevertheless, once they had attained the franchise, as our case study demonstrates, African American women in New York fought relentlessly to make the state responsive to their demands. Over the course of sixty years, they could count some notable successes that resulted from their state-centered activism. Women like Helen Holman helped women attain the vote. Others like Bessie Buchanan and Shirley Chisholm convinced male-dominated political parties to give them a chance at the polls, and then they won over voters. These are important examples of change that become apparent when we shift from a national picture, which in terms of women's equal rights to citizenship was quite bleak despite the vote, to the state and local levels, which suggested not only nuance but even some progress.

At the same time, as we have also argued, there were limits to what women could achieve nationally and in New York because of entrenched power dynamics embedded in the political culture, and because they lacked the kinds of institutional networks and partners that could readily move their goals forward. When legislative bodies and their predominantly white male leadership resisted the ideas that women, especially African American women, put forward, the heaviest price was paid by those who needed support the most and who made up the communities on whose behalf women like Holman, Buchanan, Chisholm, Ginsberg, Vinson, and Phillips were fighting. These women and many others brought about political and legal changes despite significant limits on what they were able to achieve. Such hard-won changes, in turn, helped transform the cultures (political and otherwise) that had repudiated the influence of these women on politics in the first place.

The history of women gaining citizenship rights in the United States often narrows to a single-issue struggle that culminated in the unmitigated success of suffrage. The scholarly periodization of feminist movements champions this victory narrative wherein the first wave of feminism concluded with the franchise—as if there were no political battles left to wage. This interpretation not only obscures the issues that voting rights failed to address but also privileges the national story at the expense of rich and varied state-level histories. Such a focus ignores the interplay between state and national political achievements in the decades after the Nineteenth Amendment's passage. An examination of state-centered activism, such as this study of black women in New York State, sheds light on some of the ways in which all women gained political rights on a national scale. Triumphs in state and local political contests occasionally paved the way for changes at the national level. At the same time, federal legislation and court decisions reverberated back to women in their daily lives as citizens and representatives. Federalism rests in part on the relationship between state and national governments—and so, too, did New York women's activism to gain full political participation at all levels of government after gaining the vote.

Notes

1. See, e.g., Bronaugh (1923).

2. See Stanton, Anthony, and Gage ([1881] 1985.)

3. See, e.g., *In re Grilli* (1920, 795, 796); *Commonwealth v. Welosky* (1931).

4. See *New York Age* (November 1, 1919, 1; May 28, 1921, 1; August 15, 1925, 1).

5. *People's Voice* (1946, 3); *New York Age* (October 13, 1951, 11); *Amsterdam News* (August 18, 1951, 2; July 17, 1954, 3). See Biondi (2006, 187) on Buchanan's friendship with Baker.

6. In 1954, in the Twelfth Assembly District, 16,766 women and 13,853 men were registered as Democrats. See *Annual Report of the Board of Elections of the City of New York* (1952, table VII) and *Annual Report* (1954, table VI).

7. See *New York Legislative Record and Index*, section on Individual Record Assembly Bills, for 1955–1962.

8. Respectively, *Griswold v. Connecticut* (1965), invalidating a Connecticut law prohibiting use of contraceptives; *Roe v. Wade* (1973), striking down a Texas law criminalizing abortion; and *UAW v. Johnson Controls* (1991), invalidating an employer's policy that excluded all fertile women from lead-exposure jobs in a battery manufacturing plant.

9. A comprehensive analysis of gender and the modern workplace can be found in Grossman (2016).

Works Cited

Biondi, Martha. 2006. *To Stand and Fight: The Struggle for Civil Rights in Postwar New York City*. Cambridge, MA: Harvard University Press.

Board of Elections of the City of New York. 1952. *Annual Report of the Board of Elections of the City of New York, 1952*. New York: Board of Elections of the City of New York.

Board of Elections of the City of New York. 1954. *Annual Report of the Board of Elections of the City of New York, 1954*. New York: Board of Elections of the City of New York.

Bronaugh, Minor. 1923. *Jury Service as Incidental to Grant of Women's Suffrage*. 27 Law Notes 147, 150.

Chused, Richard H. 1982. "Married Women's Property Law: 1800–1850." Geo. L. J. 71:1359.

Clemens, Elisabeth S. 1999. "Organizational Repertoires and Institutional Change: Women's Groups and the Transformation of American Politics, 1890–1920." In *Civic Engagement in American Democracy*, edited by Theda Skocpol and Morris P. Fiorina, 81–110. Washington, DC: Brookings Institution Press.

Commonwealth v. Welosky, 177 NE 656, 661 (Mass) (1931).

Congressional Record. 1969. January 14–July 28.

Cott, Nancy F. 1995. "Across the Divide: Women in Politics before and after 1920." In *One Woman, One Vote: Rediscovering the Woman Suffrage Movement*, edited by Marjorie Spruill Wheeler. Troutdale, OR: NewSage Press.

Craig v. Boren, 429 US 190 (1976).

Crisis. 1915. August 1915.

DuBois, Ellen Carol. 1997. *Harriot Stanton Blatch and the Winning of Woman Suffrage*. New Haven, CT: Yale University Press.

Family and Medical Leave Act, Pub. L. No. 103–03, 107 Stat. 6 (codified as amended at 29 USC § 2612–2654) (2012).

Frontiero v. Richardson, 411 US 677 (1973).

Goesaert v. Cleary, 335 US 464 (1948).

In re Grilli, 179 NYS 795 (1920).

Griswold v. Connecticut, 381 US 479 (1965).

Grossman, Joanna L. 2016. *Nine to Five: How Gender, Sex, and Sexuality Continue to Define the American Workplace*. Cambridge.

Hartog, Hendrik. 2002. *Man and Wife in America: A History*. Cambridge, MA: Harvard University Press.

Hine, Darlene Clark. 1989. *Black Women in White: Racial Conflict and Cooperation in the Nursing Profession, 1890–1950*. Bloomington: Indiana University Press.

Hoyt v. Florida. 368 US 57 (1961).

Lane, Layle. 1941. "Harlem: A Challenge to Democracy." *The Guild Teacher.* Box 184–2. Layle Lane Manuscript Collection, Moorland-Spingarn Research Center, Howard University.

Laws of the State of New York. 1918. Vol. 2. Albany, NY: J. B. Lyon.

Lewinson, Paul. 1963. *Race, Class, and Party: A History of Negro Suffrage and White Politics in the South.* New York: Russell and Russell.

Marshall, T. H. 1964. *Class, Citizenship, and Social Development: Essays by T. H. Marshall.*

Meritor Savings Bank v. Vinson, 477 US 57 (1986).

Murray, Pauli. 1964. "Memorandum in Support of Retaining the Amendment to H.R. 7152, Title VII (Equal Employment Opportunity) to Prohibit Discrimination in Employment Because of Sex," April 14, 1964. Papers. Series II: 1935–1984, Box 85, Folder 1485. Schlesinger Library, Radcliffe Institute for Advanced Study, Harvard University.

Murray, Pauli, and Mary O. Eastwood. 1965. "Jane Crow and the Law: Sex Discrimination and Title VII." *George Washington Law Review* 34, no. 2 (December): 232–56.

New York State Legislative Record and Index. Vols. 1955–1962.

Orr v. Orr, 440 US 268 (1979).

Osofsky, Gilbert. 1966. *Harlem: The Making of a Ghetto.* Chicago: Ivan R. Dee.

People's Voice. 1946. June 8, 1946.

Philadelphia Tribune. 1916. January 15, 1916.

Phillips v. Martin Marietta Corp., 400 US 542 (1971).

Planned Parenthood v. Casey, 505 US 833 (1992).

Pregnancy Discrimination Act, Pub. L. No. 95–155, 92 Stat. 2076 (1978).

Price Waterhouse v. Hopkins, 490 US 228 (1989).

Reed v. Reed, 404 US 71 (1971).

Roe v. Wade, 410 US 113 (1973).

Siegel, Reva B. 2002. "She the People: The Nineteenth Amendment, Sex Equality, Federalism, and the Family." *Harvard Law Review* 115, no. 4 (February): 947–1046.

Skowronek, Stephen. 1982. *Building a New American State: The Expansion of National Administrative Capacities, 1877–1920.* New York: Cambridge University Press.

Stanton, Elizabeth Cady, Susan B. Anthony, and Matilda Joslyn Gage, eds. (1881) 1985. *History of Women Suffrage.*

Title IX of the Education Amendments of 1972. Pub. L. No. 92–318, 86 Stat. 235.

UAW v. Johnson Controls, Inc., 499 US 187 (1991).

United States v. Virginia, 518 US 515, 532 (1996).

US Code. 29 USC § 206(d); USC § 2000e-17 (2012).

PART II

INTERROGATING THE PRESENT

Chapter 4

Women in State Legislatures

New York in Comparative Perspective

KIRA SANBONMATSU

Women in New York State exercise tremendous power at the ballot box today. Indeed, turnout for women in the state in the 2018 election exceeded that of men (US Census 2019). Without suffrage, the voices of New York women would be diminished and women would lack the means for holding their elected officials accountable.

Voting rights are a critical feature of democracy. But there are other consequential features of our democracy, including the ability to run for office and the quality of the representational relationship between voters and elected officials (Andersen 1996). In 2019, however, New York boasted a female US senator, Kirsten Gillibrand (D), and a female lieutenant governor, Kathy Hochul (D). Senator Gillibrand, formerly a contender for the Democratic nomination for president in 2020, took over the Senate seat of another notable woman in New York politics, Hillary Clinton, who stepped down to become secretary of state under President Barack Obama. New Yorker Alexandria Ocasio-Cortez broke onto the national stage when she defeated incumbent Queens representative Joseph Crowley in the Democratic primary and went on to win his seat in the 2018 midterms. Those midterm elections proved historic as Ocasio-Cortez was one of a record number of women elected to Congress. History was also made in New York in 2018 when Letitia James became the first black woman elected to statewide office as attorney general. Moreover, Andrea Stewart-Cousins (D), also a black woman, was elected New

York Senate majority leader in 2019, marking the first time a woman was chosen to lead a chamber of the state legislature.

According to those perhaps best positioned to evaluate its significance—women in Congress—the inclusion of women in politics is integral to policymaking and the political process (Dittmar et al. 2017). As Representative Alma Adams (D-NC) observed,

> I just want to reiterate that women need to be here, and they need to be here because everything impacts us and our families and our communities. And if we're not here, then the issues that need to be talked about the most won't be talked about. They won't be addressed. You know, they'll never get to the table. So we need to be . . . in the room, at the table, feet planted firmly under the table, so that we in fact have the kind of voice that we need to have. (Dittmar et al. 2017, 52)

Yet despite the century that has elapsed since New York women won suffrage, women are far from parity with respect to elective officeholding in the state. I begin this chapter by placing New York in the context of the fifty states with respect to the status of women in elective office. A close inspection of data on women officeholders reveals that women's progress is not inevitable. I then turn to explanations for why women continue to lag behind men. Research shows that the supply of women in this country is more than sufficient and that taking steps to recruit and support more women in politics could bring the country, including New York State, closer to gender parity in officeholding.

The Status of Women in Elective Office

In 2016, just shy of the centennial of woman suffrage in New York, Hillary Clinton became the first woman to win the presidential nomination of a major party and the first woman to win the popular vote. Though Clinton failed in her bid to become the nation's first woman president, American women mobilized after her defeat. Data from the Center for American Women and Politics (CAWP) reveals that record numbers of women ran for office in 2018. And officeholding records for women of color, as well as for all women, were shattered for Congress and state legislatures (CAWP 2018).

But women have not accomplished parity with men. Women in 2019 constitute only 25 percent of the US Senate, 23.4 percent of the US House, 27.6 percent of statewide elective executive positions, and 28.8 percent of state legislators (CAWP 2019). Just nine of the nation's fifty governors are women.

It is often assumed that women are faring better at the local level as opposed to state and national levels. But women make up only 20.9 percent of mayors of cities with a population over thirty thousand (CAWP 2019). These statistics stand in contrast to the status of women as a majority of the electorate.

In many ways, women in New York State are ahead. New York ranks sixteenth among the fifty states (see figure 4.1), with women constituting 32.4 percent of all state legislators—the highest percentage in New York history (CAWP 2019). With a female US senator and

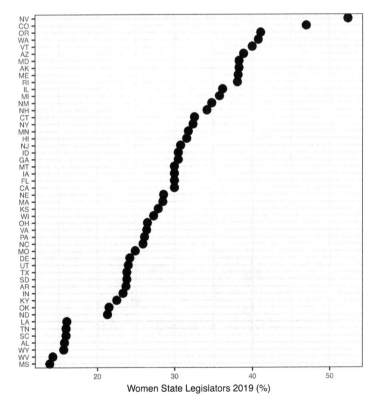

Figure 4.1. New York ranks sixteenth for women's state legislative representation. *Source:* Center for American Women and Politics. Public domain.

female lieutenant governor, New York is also ahead of the majority
of states today for women's officeholding; twenty-two other states currently send at least one woman to the US Senate and only fourteen
other states have a female lieutenant governor. At the same time,
New York lags behind on some measures. For example, the state has
yet to elect a woman governor.

Nationally, while the presence of women in elective office has
increased over the course of the past century, the two decades leading
up to the 2018 election are best characterized as a period of stagnation.
As figure 4.2 shows, while the share of women in state legislatures
increased gradually over the 1970s, a plateau was apparent in the
level of officeholding beginning in the 1990s. This stagnation period
ended with the 2018 election results, with more women serving in
state legislatures than ever before. And Nevada became the first state
to achieve a majority-female legislature in 2019.

Among all women state legislators from the two major parties,
68.6 percent are Democrats and 31.4 percent are Republicans (CAWP

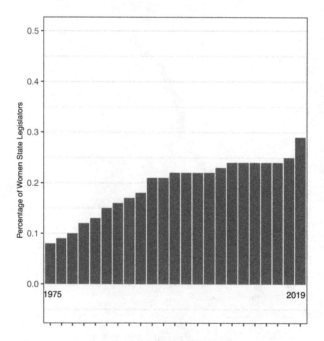

Figure 4.2. The presence of women in state legislatures increased in 2019.
Source: Center for American Women and Politics. Public domain.

2019). With a gender gap in the electorate in which women voters tend to be more likely than men to favor the Democratic Party over the Republican Party, it is not unexpected that more women elected officials would be Democratic than Republican.

Yet a striking feature about women's state legislative officeholding emerges when one adjusts for the total number of state legislators from each major party. The Republican Party controls both legislative chambers in thirty states today (National Conference of State Legislatures 2019). In contrast, only eighteen state legislatures are controlled by Democrats, with one state experiencing divided control.

Adjusting for the total number of legislators from each party makes plain an important feature of women's state legislative representation. Only 17.3 percent of today's Republican state legislators are female, whereas 41.9 percent of Democratic state legislators are female. As figure 4.3 indicates, the share of female state legislators nationally who are Republican has been stagnant, while the share who are Democratic continues to grow. These numbers mean that

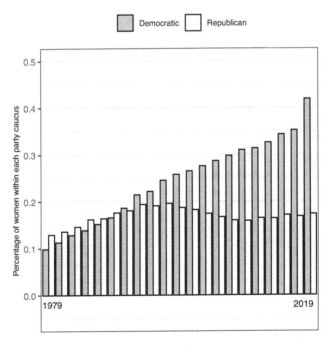

Figure 4.3. Democratic women outpace Republican women as state legislators. *Source:* Center for American Women and Politics. Public domain.

women are especially underrepresented in the party that controls most legislative chambers. A similar trend is evident in the party affiliations of members of Congress, although Republican women are even more poorly represented in Congress than in the state legislatures.

The more favorable situation for women in elective office in New York State compared to much of the country partly reflects the success of Democratic candidates. New Yorkers have selected Democratic candidates for governor, both US Senate seats, and over three-fourths of US House seats. In addition to Senator Gillibrand, about 30 percent of the congressional delegation is female. Nearly all the women elected to the House of Representatives from New York State, or eight out of nine, are Democrats (CAWP 2019). New York State is also more racially and ethnically diverse than most other states. According to the US Census, 41 percent of New Yorkers identify their backgrounds as other than non-Hispanic white (Humes, Jones, and Ramirez 2011). And there is considerable diversity among New York's female elected officials. Four of the nine women New York sends to the US House of Representatives are women of color, as are about half of female state legislators, according to CAWP's data. Virtually all these women identify as Democrats.

Nationally, we see that women of color have increased as a share of all state legislators and members of Congress (CAWP 2019). In 2019, women of color comprised 6.2 percent of all state legislators and 8.8 percent of all members of Congress; they made up 24.3 percent of all female state legislators and 37 percent of all women in Congress (CAWP 2019). The civil rights movement, the women's movement, the passage of the 1965 Voting Rights Act, and immigration reform have combined to break down many of the gender and racial barriers that had artificially deterred more diverse candidates from seeking office (Smooth 2010; Hardy-Fanta et al. 2016). The gains women of color made in New York State in 2018 were notable, including Representative Ocasio-Cortez's surprising victory, which made her the youngest woman elected to Congress. Ocasio-Cortez, who is Puerto Rican, campaigned with other women of color and helped to usher in the most diverse freshman class in the history of Congress.

Yet women of color rarely achieve statewide elective executive offices such as governor, attorney general, or secretary of state (Sanbonmatsu 2016). As the state and nation as a whole continue to become more racially and ethnically diverse, more women and men of color are poised to seek and hold elective office (Hardy-Fanta et al. 2016). While most elected officials of color are elected from communities of color, the success of individuals such as President Obama remind us that communities that are majority white can support diverse candidates.

Sources of Women's Representation and Underrepresentation

During an interview with CAWP, a female state legislator observed, "We [women] are not really ones to just throw ourselves at something if we don't think we can be successful at it . . . [But] anyone can do this, if you are willing to do the job, [and] put the time in" (Sanbonmatsu, Carroll, and Walsh 2009, 22). In short, this legislator expressed confidence that more women could successfully reach state legislatures so long as they were motivated and dedicated to the endeavor. External encouragement helps as well, according to another legislator who explained, "I think women desire to serve, have a heart to serve, but . . . sometimes they may need that little extra push" (Sanbonmatsu, Carroll, and Walsh 2009, 8).

A natural question that arises from this survey of the landscape of elected officials is what the future holds for women's officeholding. We have already seen that women are not represented in government in proportion to their presence in the population. While women's officeholding is higher today than in the past, women's gains have been uneven. And whereas we might expect that the passage of time would resolve any inequalities that women might encounter in politics, gains for women in elective office are not inevitable. Indeed, the 2018 midterm election was not a favorable one for Republican women as their numbers in Congress declined (CAWP 2018).

A comprehensive study by CAWP about pathways to state legislative office provides insight into some of the challenges that remain as well as the existence of opportunities (Carroll and Sanbonmatsu 2013). This 2008 study largely replicated one conducted by CAWP in 1981 that surveyed state legislators from all fifty states about their backgrounds and decisions about running for office. It remains the most detailed national assessment of gender differences in pathways to state legislatures.

Certainly, challenges are evident in how women reach office. For example, some women who successfully reached the legislature overcame efforts to discourage their candidacies. Of the women legislators in the study, about one-third had overcome efforts to dissuade them from seeking elective office (Sanbonmatsu, Carroll, and Walsh 2009). Women in the study were less likely than their male colleagues to have young children and they were more likely to cite the age of their children as a factor in their decision to seek office. Despite changes in the gendered division of labor in the home, women remain disproportionately responsible for caregiving (Pew Research Center 2015).

Fundraising also emerged from the study as a barrier. Despite the existence of research, largely based on congressional elections, that indicates women can raise money at levels comparable to men (Burrell 2014), the CAWP research found that female state legislators perceive gender inequality in fundraising. Most believe it is harder for women than men to raise money, in part because women do not have the same monied networks as their male colleagues (Sanbonmatsu, Carroll, and Walsh 2009). Although women have made tremendous gains in educational attainment and in the workplace, women continue to earn less than men and are less likely to be working in high-income occupations. Women's earnings, employment opportunities, and wealth also depend on race and ethnicity (IWPR 2017a, 2017b). State legislators who are women of color were especially likely to perceive gender inequalities in fundraising (Carroll and Sanbonmatsu 2013).

Alongside challenges were glimpses of opportunities available for women in politics today (Carroll and Sanbonmatsu 2013). Of the female state representatives who participated in the study, one-quarter stated that the main reason they sought their current office was because a party leader or elected official had asked them to run. Most state legislators—male and female—said that the party supported their candidacies (Sanbonmatsu, Carroll, and Walsh 2009). Thus, most women legislators reached office with party support and many sought their seat as a result of party encouragement.

One of the most important findings from the CAWP study is that women were much more likely than men to say they pursued elective office as a result of recruitment. In contrast, men were more likely to say that they ran because it was their idea (Carroll and Sanbonmatsu 2013). Research on socialization shows that women and men do not aspire to political careers at the same rates given the male-dominated nature of the occupation (Elder 2004; Lawless and Fox 2010; Shames

2017; Bos and Schneider 2016). In light of the historic exclusion of women from politics, it is understandable that women would be more likely to benefit from encouragement and the suggestion to run. Attention to the fact of women's underrepresentation can also spur women to seek office, as occurred in the 1992 and 2018 elections (Sanbonmatsu, forthcoming).

It would be a mistake to assume that women must enter politics in the same ways that men do. In fact, Carroll and Sanbonmatsu (2013, 42) argue that a "relationally embedded" model of candidacy better captures women's decision-making about candidacy than the typical ambition model in which candidacy is assumed to be self-initiated. The relationally embedded notion of candidacy arises from the reports of female state legislators who are more likely than men to take into account the perspectives of others in their decision-making process. Female state legislators were more likely to express concern about the age of their children and to voice an interest in securing party support. Women were also more likely to have obtained organizational support for their candidacies. And as previously stated, women were more likely to run as a result of someone else's suggestion. Thus, the assumption that individuals must aspire to office from a young age seems to be based on studies of how men typically reach office. Women may grow up with a desire to be in politics, and many of these women are represented in CAWP's research. But the ambition model is not the only account of office-seeking.

One important implication of the relationally embedded model of candidacy concerns inferences we can make about the future of women's officeholding. The model implies that generational change or a resocialization of American women is not necessary in order to increase the presence of women in elective office. Instead, recruiting and supporting women candidates can expand this presence.

The relationally embedded model also throws light on the party gap evident among female state legislators. Comparing the two major parties, one can see that feminist organizations and women's rights issues are typically associated with the Democratic Party (Wolbrecht 2000; Freeman 1987; Sanbonmatsu 2002). Women's organizations and political action committees provide needed infrastructure for women's candidacies. And these resources are more likely to be found on the Democratic side of the spectrum compared with the Republican side (Carroll and Sanbonmatsu 2013; Och and Shames 2018). Moreover, the greater number of Democratic women in elective office creates a larger pipeline of women for formal leadership positions within the party and within different levels of government. Having more women in leadership roles can increase the likelihood that women are recruited because personal networks are often segregated by gender (Sanbonmatsu 2006).

Party organizations can also play a vital role in encouraging more women to enter politics. Because recruitment plays a disproportionate role in women's candidacy decisions, women are more reliant on party support to be successful. This means that parties can also be negative gatekeepers to women's candidacies, as well as to men's. A national study of women's representation revealed that stronger party organizations are associated with fewer female state legislators (Sanbonmatsu 2006). The relatively strong role of parties in New York compared with other states may partly explain why women have not experienced more success. And across the country, both parties could be more inclusive in encouraging and supporting women of color as candidates.

Those interested in expanding the presence of women in politics must take parties into account. And those activists and organizations interested in women in politics might think of nontraditional places when tapping candidates. Female state legislators are more likely than their male colleagues to come from female-dominated occupations such as health and education, meaning that more male-dominated fields such as law and business are not the only pipelines to politics (Carroll and Sanbonmatsu 2013). Activists can also channel women's passion for addressing social problems into candidacy given that female state legislators were more likely than their male counterparts to run for office due to public policy concerns (Carroll and Sanbonmatsu 2013).

Conclusion

The centennial of woman suffrage in New York State provided an opportunity to take stock of how far women in the state have come in elective officeholding. Women in New York outpace women in other states in many ways. But they have not achieved gender parity. While the historic exclusion of women from politics and contemporary gender inequalities in areas such as income and social networks can make it more difficult for women to seek office, there is no reason that more women, from all racial and ethnic backgrounds and both major political parties, could not be running for and winning office today.

Works Cited

Andersen, Kristi. 1996. *After Suffrage: Women in Partisan and Electoral Politics before the New Deal*. Chicago: University of Chicago Press.

Bos, Angela L., and Monica C. Schneider, eds. 2016. *The Political Psychology of Women in U.S. Politics*. New York: Routledge.

Burrell, Barbara C. 2014. *Gender in Campaigns for the U.S. House of Representatives*. Ann Arbor: University of Michigan Press.

Carroll, Susan J., and Kira Sanbonmatsu. 2013. *More Women Can Run: Gender and Pathways to the State Legislatures*. New York: Oxford University Press.

CAWP (Center for American Women and Politics). 2018. "Results: Women Candidates in the 2018 Elections." Press release. November 29, 2018. https://cawp.rutgers.edu/press-releases.

CAWP (Center for American Women and Politics). 2019. "Fact Sheets." Accessed April 23, 2019. http://cawp.rutgers.edu/facts.

Dittmar, Kelly, Kira Sanbonmatsu, Susan J. Carroll, Debbie Walsh, and Catherine Wineinger. 2017. *Representation Matters: Women in the U.S. Congress*. New Brunswick, NJ: Center for American Women and Politics, Eagleton Institute of Politics, Rutgers University.

Elder, Laurel. 2004. "Why Women Don't Run." *Women & Politics* 26 (2): 27–56.

Freeman, Jo. 1987. "Whom You Know versus Whom You Represent: Feminist Influence in the Democratic and Republican Parties." In *The Women's Movements of the United States and Western Europe: Consciousness, Political Opportunity, and Public Policy*, edited by Mary Fainsod Katzenstein and Carol Mueller, 215–44. Philadelphia: Temple University Press.

Hardy-Fanta, Carol, Pei-te Lien, Dianne Pinderhughes, and Christine Marie Sierra. 2016. *Contested Transformation: Race, Gender, and Political Leadership in 21st Century America*. New York: Cambridge University Press.

Humes, Karen R., Nicholas A. Jones, and Roberto R. Ramirez. 2011. *Overview of Race and Hispanic Origin: 2010*. 2010 Census Briefs.

IWPR (Institute for Women's Policy Research). 2017a. *The Gender Wage Gap: 2016 Earnings Differences by Gender, Race, and Ethnicity*. Fact sheet. IWPR #C459. https://iwpr.org/publications/gender-wage-gap-2016-earnings-differences-gender-race-ethnicity/.

IWPR (Institute for Women's Policy Research). 2017b. *The Gender Wage Gap by Occupation 2016 and by Race and Ethnicity*. Fact sheet. IWPR #C456. https://iwpr.org/publications/gender-wage-gap-occupation-2016-race-ethnicity/.

Lawless, Jennifer L., and Richard L. Fox. 2010. *It Still Takes a Candidate: Why Women Don't Run for Office*. New York: Cambridge University Press.

National Conference of State Legislatures. 2019. "State Partisan Composition." Accessed October 15, 2019. http://www.ncsl.org/research/about-state-legislatures/partisan-composition.aspx.

Och, Malliga, and Shauna L. Shames, eds. 2018. *The Right Women: Republican Party Activists, Candidates, and Legislators*. Santa Barbara, CA: Praeger.

Pew Research Center. 2015. "Raising Kids and Running a Household: How Working Parents Share the Load." November 4, 2015. http://www.pewsocialtrends.org/2015/11/04/raising-kids-and-running-a-household-how-working-parents-share-the-load/.

Sanbonmatsu, Kira. 2002. *Democrats, Republicans, and the Politics of Women's Place*. Ann Arbor: University of Michigan Press.

Sanbonmatsu, Kira. 2006. *More Women Can Run: Gender and Party in the American States*. Ann Arbor: University of Michigan Press.

Sanbonmatsu, Kira. 2016. "Officeholding in the Fifty States: The Pathways Women of Color Take to Statewide Elective Executive Office." In *Distinct Identities: Minority Women in U.S. Politics*, edited by Nadia E. Brown and Sarah Allen Gershon, 171–86. New York: Routledge Press.

Sanbonmatsu, Kira. Forthcoming. "Women's Underrepresentation in the U.S. Congress." *Daedalus*.

Sanbonmatsu, Kira, Susan J. Carroll, and Debbie Walsh. 2009. *Poised to Run: Women's Pathways to the State Legislatures*. New Brunswick, NJ: Center for American Women and Politics, Eagleton Institute of Politics, Rutgers University.

Shames, Shauna L. 2017. *Out of the Running: Why Millennials Reject Political Careers and Why It Matters*. New York: New York University Press.

Smooth, Wendy. 2010. "African American Women and Electoral Politics: A Challenge to the Post-Race Rhetoric of the Obama Moment." In *Gender and Elections: Shaping the Future of American Politics*, 2nd ed., edited by Susan J. Carroll and Richard L. Fox, 165–86. New York: Cambridge University Press.

US Census. 2019. "Voting and Registration in the Election of November 2018." April 23, 2019. https://www.census.gov/data/tables/time-series/demo/voting-and-registration/p20-583.html.

Wolbrecht, Christina. 2000. *The Politics of Women's Rights: Parties, Positions, and Change*. Princeton, NJ: Princeton University Press.

Chapter 5

Women in Local Political Office
in New York State

KATHLEEN (KT) TOBIN

Since New Zealand first legalized woman suffrage in 1893, women have gone from having no national vote anywhere to having the right to vote nearly everywhere across the globe. By this measure, a century-long view certainly reveals that women's participation in the political arena has increased markedly. But political participation is not just about voting for leaders; it is also about being leaders. Leadership in all its dimensions is not easily measured. There is, however, one simple measure of the extent of formal political power held by women: the number of women in elected political office. This figure reveals that, while about half of the world's population is female (51 percent), women continue to be considerably underrepresented in positions of formal political power and authority. In 2019, at the top tiers of political power across the globe, only about one in four seats (24.5 percent) in national legislatures were held by women (IPU 2019).

For regional and local governments, the data is sparse, but where available it shows that the rate of women's officeholding is typically lower than national rates. Globally, women hold an estimated 20 percent of local government council seats, while only 5 percent of mayors worldwide are women (UCLG 2015). One explanation for these lower subnational rates is that while gender quotas for public office are increasingly common globally, they are more likely to be found at national rather than local levels, and patriarchal values are more enduring in smaller, provincial locales (UCLG 2015).

Here in the United States, of course, we have no gender quotas. Unlike elsewhere, the US gender gap in elected representation has traditionally been assumed to be wider at the national than the state level, and even narrower at local community levels. There is, however, limited empirical data available to prove or disprove this assumption (Holman 2017). Entities like the Inter-Parliamentary Union (IPU) systematically and regularly compile data on women in politics at national levels, and the Center for American Women and Politics (CAWP) at Rutgers University is a valuable resource for US state-level data and analysis, but there is no one-stop resource enumerating women's representation in local government.

In 2008, the Benjamin Center for Public Policy Initiatives (formerly the Center for Research, Regional Education, and Outreach) at SUNY New Paltz began gathering data on women in local government in New York State. This chapter will discuss why it is important to study women in local government and will detail some of our findings about women's level of representation and the roles women are attaining in local government. I will present and analyze data supporting three key findings:

- Overall, only about three in ten local government elected seats are held by women.

- The rate of women's representation varies according to the type of office, with women concentrated in positions that reflect feminine stereotypes and that have lower pay and lower prestige.

- With just under 30 percent of our elected local offices held by women, women have reached a significant critical mass milestone and, if an upward trend line continues, women in local politics will have greater opportunity to move beyond tokenism to more significantly impact governance.

Gender Matters

Historically, as noted, women have been on the political sidelines, largely excluded from governmental activities and community decision-making. Women need to gain much greater influence; winning elected political leadership is perhaps the best path for doing this. Norderval (1985, 84) asserted that "no society can afford to leave untapped half of its available talent," and simple math shows that recruiting more women to run can often nearly double the pool of potential leaders. An additional benefit of more women running and winning is the existence of visible role models for girls. Seeing women in government can activate aspirations in upcoming generations.

Proponents for more women in elected office contend that, without women in the room, certain issues are ignored or receive insufficient focus. Further, on some issues, women and men may have conflicting interests, and therefore men may not always be able to adequately represent those interests. In fact, a global survey of parliamentarians found that male leaders themselves noted significant differences in what men and women considered political priorities (IPU 2008). One British parliamentarian claimed, "I've become increasingly aware that there are issues that affect women disproportionately and that unless women pursue them nobody else will" (Childs 2002, 144). Reingold (1992) found that among state legislators in California and Arizona, 6 percent of male legislators cited women as an important constituency, in contrast to 34 percent of female legislators (quoted in Paxton and Hughes 2017, 217).

When men dominate there is less agenda-setting, policy focus, and legislative emphasis on such issues as health care, reproductive rights and contraception, gender-based violence, equal pay, parental leave, child and elder care, education, the environment, poverty, and social welfare (e.g., Childs and Withey 2004; IPU 2008; Schwindt-Bayer 2006; Taylor-Robinson and Heath 2003). Thus, the description of many of these topics is that they are "women's issues." Where women are represented in larger numbers, there is a higher probability that laws and policy related to women's issues will be passed. For example, early studies of women in government found that bills targeting children's needs and social welfare programs have a greater chance of passage when there were higher rates of elected women in legislatures (Thomas 1994). Scholars also argue that women, predisposed to more collaborative decision-making approaches, improve the political process (e.g., Eagly and Johnson 1990; Rosenthal 1998). Holman (2017) found that, compared with their male peers, female mayors of US cities focus more on women's issues and are more likely to fund social service programs. Moreover, they are more inclusive and more proactive in engaging citizens in community decision-making.

A robust democracy is achieved only when leadership is inclusive of the entire population it seeks to represent. The longtime legal and cultural exclusion of women from the public sphere thus delegitimizes allegedly democratic structures. It quiets or omits the voices of half the population affected by government's actions. Truly democratic governance incorporates the perspectives and concerns of all, especially those who have been previously marginalized by the legal system (Mansbridge 1999). A government's democratic character is measured not only by agendas and policies but also by what its composition tells us. In the words of Paxton and Hughes (2017, 4), "Looking at the makeup of political figures in a country highlights who is legitimated to make society-wide decisions in that society." Governments cannot be considered fully inclusive until women comprise approximately 50 percent of elected leadership positions. Underrepresentation of women in local elected office "may signal to women in the general population that the system is unfair, illegitimate, or biased against them" (Holman 2017, 293), and demonstrates that they, as a group, are not considered fully legitimate decision-makers in their communities.

Local Matters

One of New York's United States senators, Kirsten Gillibrand, is a woman as well as a former 2020 presidential candidate. She was appointed to the seat by governor David Paterson in 2009, when President Barack Obama appointed then-senator Hillary Clinton as US secretary of state, and was reelected twice in 2012 and 2018. Senator Clinton was elected the state's first female US senator in 2001. There has never been a female governor of the state. Kathy Hochul has been the lieutenant governor since 2015, and New York has previously had three female lieutenant governors: Mary O. Donohue (1999–2006), Elizabeth McCaughey Ross (1995–1998), and Mary Anne Krupsak (1975–1978), as well as one female secretary of state, Florence Knapp (1925–1927).

It is estimated that there are over a hundred thousand local governments with about half a million elected and appointed leaders in the United States. Simply because there are so many local governments, Darcy, Welch, and Clark (1994) concluded that most elected women serve at this level even though they are underrepresented. In New York State, the layered network of municipalities comprises nearly 1,600 local governments with elected leadership—that is, counties, cities, towns, and villages—with an estimated twelve thousand locally elected offices.[1] Additionally, and considered at least as important across the state, there are nearly five thousand elected school board members in New York (NYSSBA 2018).

Initial comparisons do not show New York to be a leader in women's representation in elected office. As Kira Sanbonmatsu reports in the previous chapter, at the statewide level in 2019, New York ranked sixteenth among all the states with 32.4 percent of statewide legislative seats held by women. But what about in local government, the level that is closest to the people? In a national study, Osborn (2012), found that about 20 percent of mayors of big cities with populations of thirty thousand or more and 19 percent of the mayors of the largest US cities were women. In 2014, only eight of the seventy-one municipalities (11.3 percent) in New York State with populations of thirty thousand or more had female mayors or supervisors (Tobin 2016). A 2008 study conducted by the Benjamin Center found that 18 percent of county legislators across the state were women. According to the National School Boards Association, 44 percent of school board members across the nation are women, but this percentage decreases with district size: in districts with enrollments of less than 2,500, women make up 34.4 percent of board members (NSBA 2016, 2018). According to the New York State School Boards Association, in 2018, 58 percent of school board members in the state were men and 42 percent were women (NYSSBA 2018).

In addition to contributing to their communities, women who are politically successful at the local level become a significant part of the pool of those who go on to be state and federal leaders. While holding previous office in local goverment is not a prerequisite for a future in a statehouse, it is a common route for both genders, as many state legislators have resumes that include previous elective or appointed political experience at lower levels. Carroll and Sanbonmatsu (2013) found that, in the US, 38.7 percent of female state representatives and 44.4 percent of their male peers held local elected office before setting their sights on state capitols. Among the women who held local offices before state legislative office, 37.1 percent served on a school board, compared with 19.9 percent of their male colleagues. About one-third (32.8 percent) of women and 43.3 percent of men with prior local service were previously elected to town or city councils. Seven percent of women and 10.4 percent of men with local government experience occupied executive positions like mayor or supervisor. About one in ten (10.9 percent of women and 11.7 percent of men) reported that their entry into public service was via their county legislature. Among the eight women newly elected to the New York State Senate in 2018, five came up through local government: Daphne Jordan (R), Town of Halfmoon councilwoman, 2014–2018; Anna Kaplan (D), Town of North Hempstead councilwoman, 2011–2018; Monica Martinez (D), Suffolk County legislator, District 9, 2014–2018; Jen Metzger (D), Town of Rosendale councilwoman, 2013–2018; and Jessica Ramos (D), Queens Community Board 3 and Assembly District 39 Democratic district leader, 2010–2014. The first female New York State Senate majority leader, Andrea Stewart-Cousins (D), previously served in the Westchester County Legislature (1996–2006).

Lastly, while election to political office at state and federal levels increasingly requires raising substantial campaign funds, running at the local level usually does not have as great a financial barrier. With respect to personal wealth, income, and access to donations, women are at an economic disadvantage. Women have less individual wealth. Moreover, for every dollar earned for full-time work by a man in 2018, a similarly employed women was paid 81.1 cents (Hegewisch and Williams-Baron 2018). Lower earnings mean that women have less money to contribute to political campaigns or to finance their own. The Institute for Women's Policy Research (2014) found that female candidates are greatly outspent compared to their male counterparts, much less likely to be large donors to political campaigns and super PACs, and more likely to support public financing for elections. Because the local level is an easier entry point when it comes to money, it is a far more feasible route into public life for those without large paychecks, fortunes, or networks of politically connected people at the ready to contribute. This is another powerful reason to pay attention to local government.

Gendered Representation

In her influential book *How Women Legislate*, Susan Thomas (1994, 30) wrote that "studying women officeholders on the local level also proved problematic . . . Accurate and complete records of women in these positions were not kept in any central clearinghouse, and the cost in time and money to carry out research on each site was overwhelming." For this research, every local government website in New York State was visited and a database of elected officials was assembled, which included information such as type of elected office and gender. Since not all local governments have websites (8 percent do not) and not all websites have information about elected leaders, adjusted estimates are reported here based on the information available in our data set of 3,944 elected local leaders.[2] Additionally reported here are some results of a 2017 survey of 384 randomly selected local elected leaders across the state.

As figure 5.1 illustrates, in New York State municipalities in 2017, 29.6 percent of the elected local government seats were occupied by women, a proportion slightly higher than the 27.7 percent in the state legislature in Albany that same year.[3] At the county level, only 16.9 percent of seats were held by women. In villages, the proportion was 25.6 percent; in cities, 30.1 percent (including 28.6 percent in New York City); and in towns, 32.7 percent. New York State is a diverse place in many ways, yet the rate of women's participation in elected office does not vary greatly across geographic regions, ranging from a low of 25.2 percent on Long Island to a high of 33.2 percent in central New York.

But just looking at overall percentages of women in local government does not tell the whole story. Gender is deeply embedded in social structure. When we examine our institutions, "the processes, practices, images and ideologies, and the distribution of power" (Acker 1992) with respect to gender become apparent. Gendered institutions reflect stereotypical expectations, and the varying placement of men and women in occupational hierarchies can reveal gender inequalities. Studies of occupational gender segregation have established that women and men are likely to have very different résumés, and part of the story is that male-dominated jobs overall provide better pay and status compared with feminized jobs (Hegewisch and Williams-Baron 2018). In the political arena, the types of offices women are more likely to pursue are associated with stereotypically feminine activities or issues like clerking and education (Rosenwasser and Dean 1989; Deckman 2007), and women are more likely to be successful getting elected to seats with less prestige (Smith, Reingold, and Owens 2011).

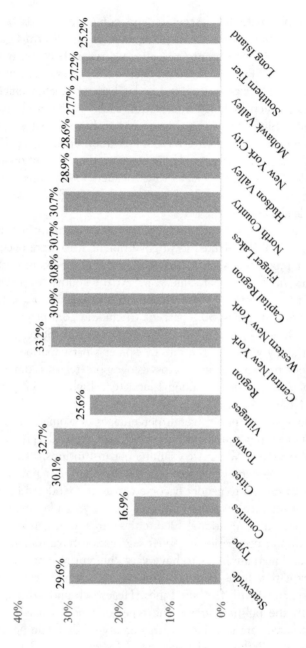

Figure 5.1. Women's rate of representation in New York State local governments by municipality. *Source:* Benjamin Center, State University of New York, New Paltz. Editors' personal archive.

In New York State's elected local governments, participation is gendered; that is, women are more likely to occupy roles that are associated with feminized tasks, lower status and prestige, and lower pay. The concentration of women in clerk positions rather than in roles like sheriff or highway superintendent illustrates this trend: 56.5 percent of county clerks and 93.1 percent of town clerks are women. In contrast, 97.4 percent of highway superintendents and 96.8 percent of sheriffs are men (see figure 5.2). Women in the state's local government offices are concentrated in jobs that are feminized, meaning associated with care and support, rather than masculinized jobs that involve law enforcement and fixing and maintaining infrastructure.

Also, the prestigious jobs at the top are dominated by men: 83.4 percent of the executive seats—which includes county executives, city and village mayors, and town supervisors—are held by men. Approximately four of every twenty-five city and village mayors and town supervisors are women. Only four of eighteen county executives (22.2 percent) are women, scattered around the state in Monroe, Nassau, Onondaga, and Putnam counties. Only one of seven (14.3 percent) county comptrollers is a woman, recently elected in Dutchess County.

Lastly, as shown in figure 5.3, women are more likely to occupy part-time seats and seats with lower pay. While less than one in five local government offices are considered full-time, the individual offices that are more likely to be full-time are more often held by men. All the county executive, county comptroller, and county sheriff seats are full-time positions, as are the vast majority of highway supervisor jobs (83.4 percent). Meanwhile, just under half (49.1 percent) of town clerk positions are part-time. Executive positions are the highest paid with 30.9 percent garnering more than $25,000 per year, and while 57.7 percent of highway superintendents make less than $50,000 annually, 82.9 percent of town clerks make less than $50,000 per year.

Critical Mass

Several scholars interested in minority power have suggested that once a certain ratio exists between a minority group and a dominating group, a threshold is reached at which the nature of the minority's power changes. Kanter (1977), who studied women in business, utilized this theory to contend that when the proportion of men is 85

Figure 5.2. Women's rate of representation in New York State local governments by office. *Source:* Benjamin Center, State University of New York, New Paltz. Editors' personal archive.

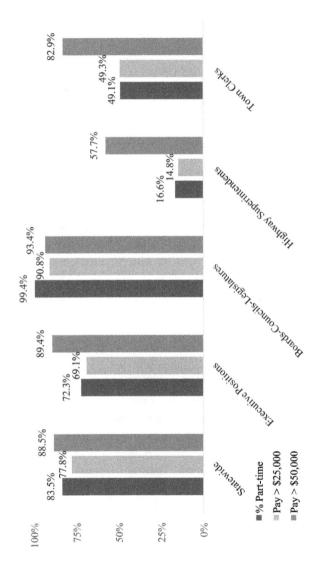

Figure 5.3. New York State local governments by office: Full- or part-time and elected pay. *Source:* Benjamin Center, State University of New York, New Paltz. Editors' personal archive.

percent or greater, women are viewed and treated as tokens without real power to initiate and execute change, and are more likely to act like the dominant type: that is, men. But, Kanter expected that the pressure to conform in male-dominated spheres would decrease as the percentage of women increased. Scholars of women in politics adopted and modified these ideas, positing that increased representation in legislative bodies would catalyze the formation of powerful coalitions among women. These coalitions would then lead to an increased focus on women's issues in legislation and legislative bodies (e.g., Childs and Krook 2008).

The magic number seems to be 30 percent. Dahlerup (1988, 281) expanded on Kanter's original findings by identifying 30 percent representation as a critical mass marker for women to create structural changes in Scandinavian politics. Quamruzzaman and Lange's (2016, 56) study demonstrated that a critical mass of women in politics was needed to get child health legislation passed in a cross section of twenty countries. In fact, in 1995, the United Nations Economic and Social Council endorsed a target of at least 30 percent women in each nation's decision-making roles. This conforms to the UN's women's leadership and political participation agenda, which asserts that 30 percent representation is necessary for women to make a visible impact (UNGA 2013).

Many New Yorkers still hold patriarchal, sexist values when it comes to women in politics. A significant portion of the public thinks that political parties and voters are generally opposed to female politicians. Many still believe that men are better at facing political pressure and are more persuasive in political office, and that male experts and sources are more trustworthy than female sources (Walter et al. 2017). This is another reason why women achieving critical mass is so important: it has the potential to change the general public's perceptions about women's ability to serve. A virtuous cycle can then be created, and providing role models can also impel an increase in the number of women engaged in political activities in general (e.g., High-Pippert and Comer 1998; Atkeson 2003).

Currently, about 30 percent of the state's local elected representatives are women, with women constituting 27.4 percent of legislative seats on town and village boards, on city councils, and in county legislatures. Although still quite outnumbered, a critical mass of women in local politics opens the door to greater impacts. The effect that critical mass has on actually changing the types of actions legislatures take is debated and still somewhat unknown due to mixed evidence in widely varying contexts. And the increase in women's relative power may not take a linear path because it often causes backlashes against significant changes in power structure (Paxton and Hughes 2017). But at a minium, achieving the tipping point in the proportion of women in these offices can change perceptions about the appropriateness of women in political office (Norris 1993).

Conclusion

The Center for American Women and Politics reported that in 2018 there were more women running for state and federal offices than ever before, easily breaking previous records. Right now in New York State, while women are certainly underrepresented and participation is clearly gendered, with just shy of 30 percent of local elected offices held by women, the state is at an important threshold moment for empowering locally elected women already in office and for generating greater interest among women to decide to run for these offices. It is certainly a significant breakthrough in state politics that locally elected women have cumulatively hit this milestone. With this baseline measured, the Benjamin Center will continue to monitor the rate of women's representation in local government and to assess policy and legislative impacts.

Notes

1. There are some other elected local government seats, such as on fire districts and water boards, but these are outside of the scope of this research and typically involve very low citizen attention and voter turnout.

2. We also wish to thank Chris Anderson of the Association of Towns of the State of New York and Haley Viccaro of the New York Conference of Mayors, who helped us fill in some data gaps.

3. We sought to utilize an intersectional lens in this analysis, but race and ethnicity are not easy to assess based on the available information on local government websites. And the number of nonwhite respondents in our survey was extremely low: 96 percent were white and less than 1 percent were Hispanic/Latinx, African American or black, Asian, or Native American.

Works Cited

Acker, Joan. 1992. "From Sex Roles to Gendered Institutions." *Contemporary Sociology* 21, no. 5 (September): 565–69.

Atkeson, Lonna Rea. 2003. "Not All Cues Are Created Equal: The Conditional Impact of Female Candidates on Political Engagement." *Journal of Politics* 65, no. 4 (November): 1040–61.

Carroll, Susan J., and Kira Sanbonmatsu. 2013. *More Women Can Run: Gender and Pathways to the State Legislatures.* Oxford: Oxford University Press.

CAWP (Center for American Women and Politics). 2018. "Data Point: 2018, A Year of the Woman Like 1992?" January 23, 2018. http://cawp.rutgers. edu/sites/default/files/resources/data-point-compare-1992-2018.pdf.

Childs, Sarah. 2002. "Hitting the Target: Are Labour Women MP's 'Acting For' Women?" *Parliamentary Affairs* 55, no. 1 (January):143–53.

Childs, Sarah, and Mona Lena Krook. 2008. "Critical Mass Theory and Women's Political Representation." *Political Studies* 56, no. 3 (October): 725–36.

Childs, Sarah, and Julie Withey. 2004. "Women Representatives Acting for Women: Sex and the Signing of Early Day Motions in the 1997 British Parliament." *Political Studies* 52, no. 3 (October): 552–64.

Dahlerup, D. 1988. From a Small to a Large Minority: Women in Scandinavian Politics. *Scandinavian Political Studies*, 11 (December): 275–98.

Darcy, Robert, Susan Welch, and Janet Clark. 1994. *Women, Elections, and Representation.* 2nd ed. Lincoln: University of Nebraska Press.

Deckman, Melissa Marie. 2007. "Gender Differences in the Decision to Run for School Board." *American Politics Research* 35, no. 4 (July): 541.

Eagly, Alice H., and Blair T. Johnson. 1990. "Gender and Leadership Style: A Meta-analysis." *Psychological Bulletin* 108, no. 2 (September): 233–56.

Hegewisch, Ariane, and Emma Williams-Baron. 2018. *The Gender Wage Gap by Occupation 2018 and by Race and Ethnicity.* Institute for Women's Policy Research. https://iwpr.org/wp-content/uploads/2019/04/C480_The-Gender-Wage-Gap-by-Occupation-2018-1.pdf.

High-Pippert, Angela, and John Comer. 1998. "Female Empowerment: The Influence of Women Representing Women." *Women & Politics* 19 (4): 53–66.

Holman, Mirya R. 2017. "Women in Local Government: What We Know and Where We Go From Here." *State and Local Government Review* 49, no. 4 (September): 285–96.

Institute for Women's Policy Research. 2014. *Money in Politics with a Gender Lens.* January 2014. https://www.icrw.org/publications/money-in-politics-with-a-gender-lens/.

IPU (Inter-Parliamentary Union). 2008. *Equality in Politics: A Survey of Women and Men in Parliaments*. Reports and Documents no. 54. http://archive. ipu.org/PDF/publications/equality08-e.pdf.

IPU (Inter-Parliamentary Union). 2019. "Women in National Parliaments: Situation as of 1st September 2019." Accessed November 4, 2019. http:// archive.ipu.org/wmn-e/arc/world010919.htm.

Kanter, Rosabeth M. 1977. *Men and Women of the Corporation*. New York: Basic Books.

Mansbridge, Jane. 1999. "Should Blacks Represent Blacks and Women Represent Women? A Contingent 'Yes.'" *Journal of Politics* 61, no. 3 (August): 628–57.

Norderval, Ingunn. 1985. "Party and Legislative Participation among Scandinavian Women." *Women and Politics in Western Europe* 18 (4): 71–89.

Norris, Pippa. 1993. "Conclusions: Comparing Legislative Recruitment." In *Gender and Party Politics*, edited by J. Lovenduski and P. Norris, 309–30. Newbury Park, CA: Sage.

NSBA (National School Boards Association). 2016, 2018. https://www. nsba.org/about-us/frequently-asked-questions, June 2016 and February 13, 2018.

NYSSBA (New York State School Boards Association). 2018. "NYSSBA Overview." Accessed March 21, 2018. http://www.nyssba.org/about-nyssba/ nyssba-overview/.

Osborn, Tracy. 2012. *How Women Represent Women: Political Parties, Gender, and Representation in the State Legislatures*. New York: Oxford University Press.

Paxton, Pamela, and Melanie Hughes. 2017. *Women, Politics, and Power: A Global Perspective*. 3rd ed. Los Angeles: CQ Press/Sage.

Quamruzzaman, Amm, and Matthew Lange. 2016. "Female Political Representation and Child Health: Evidence from a Multilevel Analysis." *Social Science and Medicine* 171 (December): 48–57.

Rosenthal, Cindy Simon. 1998. "Determinants of Collective Leadership: Civic Engagement, Gender, or Organizational Norms?" *Political Research Quarterly* 51, no. 4 (December): 847–68

Rosenwasser, Shirley, and Norma Dean. 1989. "Gender Role and Political Office: Effects of Perceived Masculinity/Femininity of Candidate and Political Office." *Psychology of Women Quarterly* 13:77–85.

Schumaker, Paul, and Nancy Burns. 1988. "Gender Cleavages and the Resolution of Local Policy Issues." *American Journal of Political Science* 32:1070–95.

Schwindt-Bayer, Leslie A. 2006. "Still Supermadres? Gender and the Policy Priorities of Latin American Legislators." *American Journal of Political Science* 50, no. 3 (July): 570–85.

Smith, Adrienne R., Beth Reingold, and Michael Leo Owens. 2012. "The Political Determinants of Women's Descriptive Representation in Cities." *Political Research Quarterly* 65, no. 2 (June): 315–29.

Taylor-Robinson, Michelle M., and Roseanna Michelle Heath. 2003. "Do Women Legislators Have Different Policy Priorities Than Their Male Colleagues? A Critical Case Test." *Women and Politics* 24, no. 4 (January): 77–101.

Thomas, Sue. 1994. *How Women Legislate*. Oxford: Oxford University Press.

Tobin, Kathleen. 2016. "Gender: Impacts on Participation in Local Government." PhD diss., State University of New York at Albany.

UCLG (United Cities and Local Governments). 2015. *The Role of Local Governments in Promoting Gender Equality for Sustainability*. December 6, 2015. https://www.uclg.org/sites/default/files/the_role_of_local_governments_in_promoting_gender_equality_for_sustainability.pdf.

UNGA (United Nations General Assembly). 2013. *Measures Taken and Progress Achieved in the Promotion of Women and Political Participation: Report of the Secretary-General*. July 24, 2013. https://digitallibrary.un.org/record/755820.

Walter, Eve, Robin Jacobowitz, Kathleen Dowley, and L. Huddy. 2017. View on Women, Women@Work Poll.

Chapter 6

New Yorkers' Views on Women and Politics One Hundred Years after State Suffrage

KATHLEEN M. DOWLEY AND EVE WALTER[1]

"In the hands of women will lie the balance of power."

—Mary Lilly, New York State Assemblywoman, 1918

As the previous chapters in this volume make clear, while New York was not the first state in the union to ratify woman suffrage, it was at the center of the movement in the early twentieth century, and many of the best-known leaders of the movement hailed from New York State, from Sojourner Truth to Susan B. Anthony to Matilda Joslyn Gage to Carrie Chapman Catt. But though New York women were at the forefront of the state and national movements for suffrage, translating that activism and training into increased political representation for the women of New York was a longer time coming. Though two women active in the suffrage movement were elected to serve in the 1919 New York State Assembly, Ida Sammis (R) and Mary M. Lilly (D), it was not until nearly a decade later that New York elected its first woman, Ruth Sears Baker Pratt (R), to serve in its national congressional delegation. A total of thirty-six women entered the US Congress from 1935 to 1954, four of whom were from New York, including the long-serving representatives Katherine Price Collier (R, 1947–1965) and Edna Flannery Kelly (D, 1949–1969).[2]

In 1969, the first African American woman, Shirley Chisolm (D), was elected to Congress from New York and went on to serve until 1983. She was also the first woman to try to secure the Democratic nomination for president. Bella Abzug (D, 1971–1987), Elizabeth Holtzman (R, 1973–1981), and Geraldine Ferraro (D, 1979–1985) joined her in the New York congressional delegation before Ferraro stepped down to accept the Democratic nomination for vice president on the ill-fated Walter Mondale ticket. Although no women from New York were elected in the Ninety-Ninth Congress (1985–1987), Louise Slaughter (D), Nita M. Lowey (D), and Susan Molinari (R) went on to serve lengthy terms and were eventually joined by Caroline Maloney (D) and Nydia Velazquez (D). In 1997, when New York voters additionally elected Sue Kelly (R) and Carolyn McCarthy (D), they made the New York delegation one of the most gender-balanced in the country, albeit still nowhere near parity (seven out of thirty-one seats, or 23 percent).

Following the 2016 election, New York had nine women in a reduced delegation of twenty-seven (33 percent), with Claudia Tenney (R), Kathleen Rice (D), Elise Stefanik (R), Grace Meng (D), and Yvette Clark (D) joining the long-serving Lowey, Maloney, Slaughter, and Velazquez. Representative Slaughter passed away during the winter of 2018, after three decades in Congress, having served as the first woman chair of the powerful Rules Committee. As one of the longest-serving women in the House of Representatives, Slaughter was a prominent voice for women and diversity. She was a founding member and co-chair of the Congressional Pro-Choice Caucus, wrote and successfully fought for the passage of legislation that guarantees women and minorities are included in all federal health trials, established the Office of Research on Women's Health at the National Institutes of Health, and coauthored the 1994 landmark Violence Against Women Act (Press Release on the Passing of Louise Slaughter, https://louise.house.gov/media-center/press-releases/statement-passing-congresswoman-louise-m-slaughter). Despite the overall increase in the number of women elected to Congress in the 2018 midterms, including the highly publicized victory of Alexandria Ocasio-Cortez, New York's delegation now has eight women in its twenty-seven-person delegation (30 percent).

The Center for American Women and Politics (CAWP) reports that only California has sent more women to Congress than New York, and while there are several states that have sent a higher percentage of their delegation to Washington (New Hampshire, for example, became famous after 2016 for sending an all-female delegation), most of those states have very small congressional delegations (like New Hampshire, with two representatives). New York has also had two female senators: Hillary Rodham Clinton and incumbent Kirsten Gillibrand, both Democrats. At the state level, as Kira Sanbonmatsu reports in her earlier chapter, New York did make gains in 2018, advancing from twentieth to sixteenth in women in state elective office (CAWP 2017).

The 2016 Presidential Election and New Yorkers' Views on Women in Politics

Former New York senator Hillary Clinton's successful campaign to win the Democratic nomination for president seemed to coincide with the initial public conversations in commemoration of the centennial of woman suffrage in New York and provided significant momentum for and interest in examining public attitudes about women in politics in New York State. Given the tremendous legacy of long-term women legislators in New York, from Shirley Chisolm to Bella Abzug and Geraldine Ferraro to Louise Slaughter, we sought to understand whether the comparatively lengthy history of women in legislative (albeit not executive) roles had succeeded in producing more favorable views on women in politics and greater support for legislation that is still necessary to help women achieve full and equal citizenship in the state.

In this context, and with these specific questions in mind, together with the support of the Albany-based *Times Union* news organization, we designed and launched a survey to evaluate public attitudes about women, work, and politics in New York, called the Women@Work View on Women (VOW) poll (Walter 2017). The 1,050-person online poll was fielded in November 2016, just after the election, with the goal of measuring New Yorkers' views on women, politics, and public policy, but also hoping for some insights into the shocking result of that election, the Trump victory and the Clinton defeat.

The historic 2016 presidential contest, featuring two New Yorkers and the first woman to have secured a major party nomination, was impossible to ignore in trying to understand New Yorkers' views on women. While we were interested in attitudes about women and in differences between men and women regarding public policies that predominantly affect women, we could not help but also ask about the election that had just taken place. Past research has demonstrated that in every presidential election since 1996, a persistent gender gap has emerged at the national level, with a majority of women voting for the Democratic nominee (CAWP 2017). CAWP defines the gender gap as the "difference between the percentage of women and the percentage of men voting for a given candidate, generally the winning candidate."

The national gender gap persisted in the 2016 election between Clinton and Trump, with only 41 percent of women voting nationally for the Republican nominee, Donald Trump, compared to 52 percent of men, for an 11 percent gap. Ironically, it was the largest such gap since the 1996 campaign between Bill Clinton and Bob Dole. Table 6.1 shows how the gap in New York compares to the national gap, with self-reported voting data from the fall 2016 VOW poll.

While the gender gap is notably smaller in "blue" New York, this is in large part because both men and women in the majority reported voting for Democratic candidate Hillary Clinton. A majority of both women and men voted for Hillary Clinton in all three regions (New York City, New York City Suburbs, and Upstate) as well, though the New York City margin was highest, with 78 percent of women in the city voting for Clinton while 65 percent of men did the same. Broken

Table 6.1. New York's Gender Gap in the 2016 Presidential Election

2016 Presidential Candidate	Women	Men	Gender Gap
Donald Trump (R)	33.7% (222)	37.2% (202)	3.5%
Hillary Clinton (D)	57.5% (130)	53.3% (141)	
Others (Stein/Johnson)	8.8% (34)	9.5% (36)	

down by race, we still see a slim 51 percent majority of white women voting for Clinton (unlike the national figure which saw an equally slender majority of white women voting for Trump), with 98 percent of self-identified black women, 84 percent of Latina women, and 60 percent of Asian women reporting that they voted for her. While it is clear from the past seven presidential contests that majorities of both men and women have consistently chosen the Democratic candidate in New York, women have done so at a higher rate, and with Secretary Clinton's candidacy, the gap (while smaller) persisted.

In the broader literature on women's representation, scholars have highlighted a number of important factors that contribute to greater numbers of women getting elected to national office. One of these considerations is what Paxton and Hughes (2017) refer to as the "supply" and "demand" for female candidates. While globally, the focus of late has been on the role of political institutions, especially the adoption of legislation (in over a hundred countries) establishing gender quotas in elections to national legislatures, in the United States, quotas have never seriously been considered. Moreover, at the national level, the nature of the party system (with its reliance on primaries) makes the use of such measures problematic without broader institutional change, even if the political will or taste for such measures exist.

Beyond quotas, a second set of factors related to the success or failure to increase women's political representation in the United States focuses on the high cost of campaigns, especially in a weak party system where much of the burden for financing falls largely on individual candidates. While recent research suggests women can and do raise money at rates equal to men once becoming their party's nominees (Burrell 2014), it may well be that the perception of prohibitive costs dissuades many qualified women from running. Indeed, the candidate-centered nature of US campaigns (a function of the presidential system as well as the single-member district and plurality electoral system) means there are fewer opportunities for women to make huge gains in any given election year. National-level incumbency rates in the United States are so high that there are too few "open seats" in which women could compete to challenge the status quo. As Lawless and Fox (2018, 32) have reported, in 2016, 394 of 435 representatives (91 percent) ran for reelection, and of those who ran, only thirteen lost. The midterms in 2018 produced 33 defeats among the 378 who ran, the lowest incumbency rate (91 percent) for the House since 2012 when 10.2 percent were defeated. This most recent midterm also recorded the highest number of incumbents choosing not to run again since 1992, the last such proclaimed "year of the woman" election, in which the mobilization of female anger at the treatment of Anita Hill during the confirmation hearing of Supreme Court nominee Clarence Thomas was channeled into the recruitment and election of more women.

In contrast to the prior two strands of research that focus on the underlying structural factors that make it difficult for women to overcome the deficit in their representation levels in the United States, a third strand focuses on the role of public attitudes and perceptions about women in politics, which may well explain both why so few women are running (women have less political ambition) and why political party leadership and party gatekeepers seem less inclined to recruit more women to run (voters are not seen as demanding more women's representation). Dolan and Lynch (2015, 111) assert that one of the "enduring questions asked by scholars who study women candidates in the USA," is determining "whether, when, and how public attitudes toward women shape political outcomes." In their study of voting behavior in the 2010 US House elections, they found that "attitudes about women in politics had a limited impact on voting for women candidates," but that "women and men voters are not influenced in the same way."

The challenge for the "attitudes and beliefs matter" explanations for the slowed growth of women's representation in politics is that most national surveys suggest that national attitudes about women in politics *have* changed over time and are now seen as generally supportive of the increased representation of women in politics. Dolan and Lynch (2015, 112), for example, report that according to American National Election Surveys, in 1972 only 47 percent of people agreed that women should have a larger role in public life, while in 2008 this nearly doubled to 84 percent. And the General Social Survey conducted in the United States reveals that the percentage of respondents who say the country would be governed better if there were more women in elected office rose from 33 percent in 1975 to 60 percent in 2000.

While a majority nationwide support increasing the role of women in public life, this is not tantamount to saying that more should be done by the major national political parties, the states, or the federal government to ensure that this happens. Indeed, it may well be that liberal American political culture supports the idea that women should be able to choose a career in politics. But the majority may also believe that the choice is one that women can now make as freely as men and therefore the playing field is level. Voters may now believe that when women won suffrage in New York State, or three years later nationwide, the last legal obstacle to their full participation (and access to representative office) had been lifted. While acknowledging that for women of color, the choice of politics might have necessitated several decades more of struggle, culminating in the Civil Rights Acts (1960, 1964, 1968) and the Voting Rights Act (1965), it could well be that most Americans (and New Yorkers) now believe lower levels of representation of women reflect a "natural" order (that is, women are not as interested in such a career choice). Moreover, many may conclude that a lack of descriptive representation is not a problem to confront, because they believe that men who identify as supportive of women's rights can represent women's interests just as well as women.

Feminist theorists like Jane Mansbridge (1999) have long suggested that the goal of greater descriptive representation in American democracy for women and African Americans is a legitimate and just goal, given that both women and African Americans were once deemed unfit for full citizenship by the state, but it is equally plausible that the broader public has not reached the same conclusion. And while Congresswoman Louise Slaughter's record cited above suggests that women may well substantively better represent women (on domestic violence) or at least ensure that women are not overlooked in what might appear to be gender-neutral legislation (on medical/clinical trials), again, the wider voting public may still not see a pressing need to make sure that more women in New York get elected.

As Dolan and Sanbonmatsu (2009) note, very little empirical attention has focused on the public's view of the need for greater descriptive representation of women in politics, for either normative justice reasons (past exclusion) or substantive ones (women will better represent issues that are of most concern to women). One exception is a 2014 survey of women and leadership done by the PEW Research Center, which asked multiple questions about the importance of greater representation of women in politics. But in that national survey, only

38 percent responded that they hoped "the United States would elect a female president in their lifetime," and 57 percent said it did not matter (Lawless and Fox 2018, 34).

With this information in mind, the 2016 VOW poll asked New Yorkers, "How important is it to you to increase the number of women elected to Congress?" Figure 6.1 breaks down the results by sex, political party, and recent presidential voting, identifying the percentage that responded it was very or extremely important to do so. While just over half of New York women responded this way, only 36 percent of men did so, a 16 percent gender gap in preferences.

By party affiliation, the margins are even more dramatic, with 26 percent of Republicans saying it is very or extremely important to elect more women, compared to 62 percent of Democrats in our sample, nearly a 37 percent partisan gap. By votes for president, just over 66 percent of Clinton voters expressed the belief that it was very or extremely important to elect more women, compared to 28 percent for Trump voters, the largest margin of the three comparisons at 38 percent.

It is possible that electing more women to office is not a high priority for many, because New Yorkers already believe that women have as much influence in politics today as men, despite lower levels of descriptive representation at the local, state, and national levels. We also asked, "In general, do women have more, less or about the same amount of influence in American politics as men," and the results appear below in figure 6.2. While fewer than 50 percent of men believe women have somewhat or much less influence, over 60 percent of women believe so; this gender gap is slightly larger than the partisan gap, as 48 percent of Republicans versus 57 percent of Democrats believe the same.

When asked if they thought women were less well represented than men because "the political parties and voters are opposed to female candidates," nearly 50 percent of women and 40 percent of men agreed or strongly agreed. Of course, it may be that New Yorkers believe women are just not interested in positions of such responsibility, that they perhaps lack the kind of ambition that would lead one to a career in politics. In response to a question about whether "women are less interested than men in positions of responsibility," 43 percent of men agreed with the sentiment; only 22 percent of women did so.

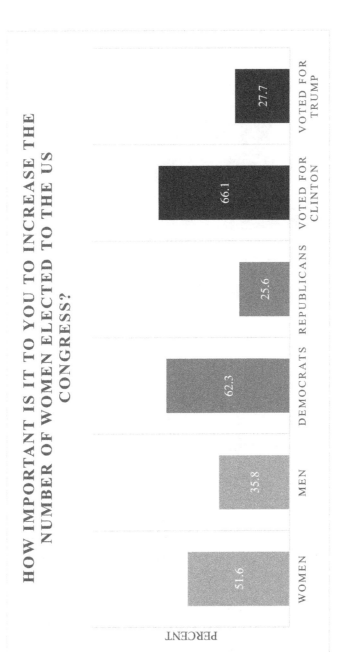

Figure 6.1. It is very or extremely important to elect more women by gender, party, and voting behavior. *Source: View on Women poll. Women@Work, Times Union.* Editors' personal archive.

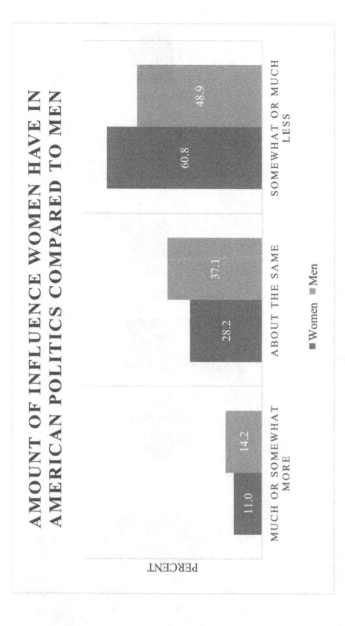

Figure 6.2. Amount of influence women have in politics. *Source:* View on Women poll. Women@Work, *Times Union.* Editors' personal archive.

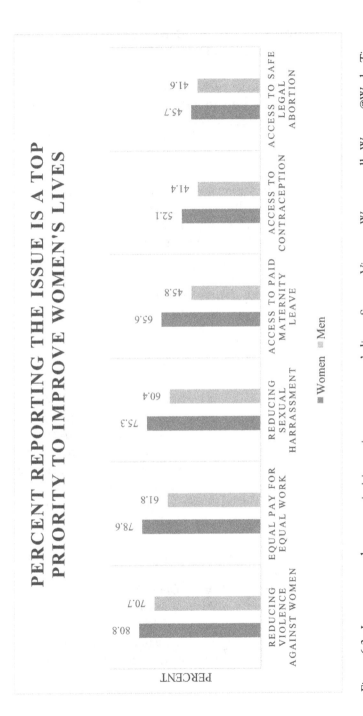

Figure 6.3. Issues reported as top priorities to improve women's lives. *Source:* View on Women poll. Women@Work, *Times Union*. Editors' personal archive.

Issues That Mattered to Women
in New York in 2016

In a series of questions designed to capture the policies that New Yorkers think are most necessary to improve women's lives, one hundred years after woman suffrage was won in the state, we asked about everything from violence against women to access to contraception and safe and legal abortion.

A persistent gender gap exists for all the issues, but the largest differences in the priorities of men and women in New York pertain to access to paid maternity leave (20 percent), equal pay for equal work (17 percent), and reducing sexual harassment (15 percent). In each case, double the number of men compared to women reported that these are "not too important."

As a follow up, we then asked respondents whether the government should help ensure that women have access to paid leave and to safe, affordable daycare. Majorities of both men and women agreed or strongly agreed that the government should do more, but the gap persists, with 89 percent of women agreeing with regard to paid leave and 84 percent with regard to childcare, compared to 76 percent and 73 percent of men, respectively. And while it is heartening that such large majorities of both men and women agree that more should be done in these areas, the gender gap suggests these are still bigger issues for women than for men; that gap is larger than the one between self-identified black and white respondents and Republicans and Democrats. This suggests that for this whole host of policy questions, with overwhelming preference for more government action, electing more women to office is likely to generate action on these top priority issues, compared to electing more men or even more Democrats.

Asking what keeps women from achieving full equality, "their own decisions, persistent discrimination, or both," yielded mixed results, which are reported below in figure 6.4, broken down by sex, partisanship, and race. Republicans are most likely to suggest that it is the choices women make (more than discrimination) that keep women from achieving true equality, while self-identified black respondents and Democrats are most likely to report discrimination as the biggest factor.

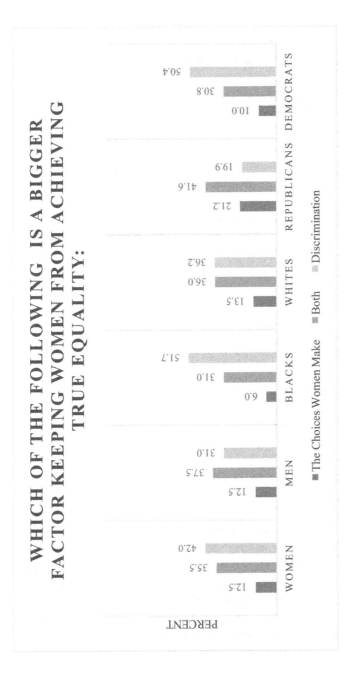

Figure 6.4. Factors preventing women from achieving equality. *Source:* View on Women poll. Women@Work, *Times Union.* Editors' personal archive.

A New York *Feminist* State of Mind?

In their book *Women, Men, and U.S. Politics*, published following the 2016 election, Jennifer Lawless and Richard Fox (2018) reflect on what the election of Donald Trump and, perhaps more consequentially, the defeat of Hillary Clinton (in the Electoral College) say about the state of feminism in the United States. While noting that there are reasons to be optimistic, including the mobilization of so many women activists for the Women's March in January of 2017, EMILY's List (2018) reporting that record numbers of women contacted them about running for office, and the historic number of women who challenged men in primaries and won in the 2018 midterm elections, Lawless and Fox find the "glass for feminism going forward three quarters empty and one quarter full" (17). Margaret Talbot (2018) noted in the *New Yorker* that "472 women have filed to run for the House in midterm elections," far surpassing the previous high of 298 in 2012. The majority of these were Democratic candidates, and clear majorities additionally support what have been identified (by Lawless and Fox and others) as feminist policies, such as those in figure 6.3: access to contraception, access to safe and legal abortion, paid maternity leave, equal pay for equal work, and a reduction in both sexual harassment and domestic violence.

When asked specifically whether they would "best describe" themselves as a feminist, only 16 percent of our sample of New York women, and 7 percent of men were willing to do so (11.5 percent overall). And though a clear majority of both men (56 percent) and women (66 percent) said they believe in equality for men and women, they did not describe themselves as feminists. But only 6 percent of men and 2 percent of women said they were "opposed" to feminism, with another 4 percent reporting that it was "irrelevant" today. Reflecting on New Yorkers' views on women and politics, roughly a hundred years following the successful state campaign for woman suffrage and on the verge of the national centennial of the same, we are left in 2020 with the impression that while much has been accomplished in terms of women's equality—including New Yorkers' preference for more state action in the areas of paid leave, access to affordable childcare, access to safe and legal means to prevent and end pregnancies, and the continued need to strengthen and enforce laws to combat sexual harassment and violence against women—there remains much work to be done.

We consider these remaining policy priorities the unfinished agenda of the liberal suffrage movement, as they represent in no small part what it is that women need in order to achieve full citizenship in New York State and in the United States more broadly. And while legislative victories for the Republican-controlled House, Senate, and presidency were few and far between from 2016 to 2018, and a newly empowered Democratic Congress seems poised to keep further rollbacks in check in during 2019–2020, the administration has had enormous success in revamping the federal judiciary, foremost among them the Supreme Court. Title IX protections, the Violence Against Women Act, reproductive rights, and voting rights are being challenged nationally once again. While New York State, with its Democratic governor, Democratic majorities in the assembly and senate, and favorable public attitudes about women and a women's equality agenda, seems poised to resist these threats to equal citizenship, not all women will be equally protected by these state-level defenses. Poor women, immigrant women, and especially undocumented women remain less protected because of federal-level policies and gaps in state-level protections.

Notes

1. We would like to thank SUNY New Paltz student Yasmine Aziz for her research assistance with this chapter.

2. For a complete list, see "Women Representatives and Senators by State and Territory, 1917–Present," at the History, Art & Archives website of the US House of Representatives: http://history.house.gov/Exhibitions-and-Publications/WIC/Historical-Data/Women-Representatives-and-Senators-by-State-and-Territory/.

Works Cited

Burrell, Barbara C. 2014. *Gender in Campaigns for the U.S. House of Representatives*. Ann Arbor: University of Michigan Press.

CAWP (Center for American Women and Politics). 2017. *The Gender Gap: Voting Choices in Presidential Elections*. http://www.cawp.rutgers.edu/sites/default/files/resources/ggpresvote.pdf.

Dolan, Kathleen, and Timothy Lynch. "Making the Connection? Attitudes about Women in Politics and Voting for Women Candidates." *Politics, Groups, and Identities* 3 (1): 111–32.

Dolan, Kathleen, and Kira Sanbonmatsu. "Gender Stereotypes and Attitudes toward Gender Balance in Government." *American Politics Research* 37, no. 3 (May): 409–28.

EMILY's List. 2018. "36,000 Women Want to Run for Office." Press Release, April 16, 2018. https://www.emilyslist.org/news/entry/36000-women-want-to-run-for-office.

Lawless, Jennifer, and Richard L. Fox. 2018. *Women, Men, and U.S. Politics: Ten Big Questions.* New York: W. W. Norton.

Mansbridge, Jane. 1999. "Should Blacks Represent Blacks and Women Represent Women? A Contingent 'Yes.'" *Journal of Politics* 61, no. 3 (August): 628–57.

Paxton, Pamela, and Melanie Hughes. 2017. *Women, Politics, and Power: A Global Perspective.* 3rd ed. Los Angeles: CQ Press/Sage.

Pew Research Center. 2015. *Women and Leadership.* January 14, 2015. http://www.pewsocialtrends.org/2015/01/14/women-and-leadership/.

Talbot, Margaret. 2018. "The Women Running in the Midterms during the Trump Era." *New Yorker*, April 18, 2018. https://www.newyorker.com/news/news-desk/2018-midterm-elections-women-candidates-trump.

Walter, E. 2017. View on Women (VOW) Poll [Data set]. Producer, *Times Union* Women@Work.

PART III

IMAGINING THE FUTURE

Chapter 7

The Limits of Woman Suffrage and the Unfinished Business of Liberal Feminism[1]

AMY R. BAEHR

The right to vote in New York State was achieved in 1917, through the hard work of activists and three years ahead of the country as a whole. This right should be understood as part of a set of essential legal rights that includes the right to own personal property, the right to equality of opportunity in education and the workplace, the right to procreative self-determination, the right to not be coercively steered into society's preferred gender roles, and the right to be free from violence. The right to vote and the right to own property were major victories of the first wave of the women's movement (roughly 1848–1920).[2] In both cases, New York was among the leading states. With respect to property, for example, New York's Married Women's Property Act (1848) was an early model (Stansell 2010). The agenda of the women's movement's second wave (beginning roughly 1966) includes codification and enforcement of all of these legal rights. It remains unfinished business. To appreciate this unfinished business, I suggest that we understand women's rights in the light of the purposes they serve, that is, in the light of the reasons why they are worthy objects of struggle. I also argue, however, that a women's rights agenda must be supplemented with a demand for fairness. Society must not be a scheme rigged to benefit some at the expense of others; individuals must enjoy their fair share of the benefits and shoulder their fair share of the burdens of social life (Rawls 1971).[3] This demand for fairness focuses our attention on the current unfair distribution of caregiving burdens in the United States, that is, on the pattern of disadvantage perpetuated by the current organization of caregiving—a pattern of disadvantage that disproportionately affects women, especially poor women, women of color, and immigrant women. While liberal feminism has long been associated with women's rights, an adequate liberal feminist agenda for the women's movement going forward must supplement a focus on women's rights with a demand for fairness in caregiving.

Women's Legal Rights in the Light of the Purposes They Serve

In this section, I discuss a women's rights agenda. I suggest that we can appreciate the significance of a women's rights agenda, and obtain a rich account of its unfinished business, if we explore women's rights in the context of the purposes they serve—that is, in the light of an account of why they are worthy of struggle.

Consider the right to vote. The legal recognition of women's right to vote in New York (1917) and in the United States generally (1920)—the result of decades of activism—was a major accomplishment. But we must not overlook the fact that the 1920 victory did not actually secure the vote for all women. Nationally, many African American and Native American women remained effectively unable to vote for additional decades; it took further activism for the law to address these racist exclusions (Roediger 2008, 171). To this day, there is suppression of the minority vote—and that means the women's vote (Berman 2016).[4]

We can appreciate the importance of the right to vote if we consider why it is worthy of struggle. I contend that one crucial reason is that the right to vote makes it possible for women to live under conditions and rules of which they are coauthors, rather than under conditions and rules men make for them. Being such a coauthor is one way to understand what it means to be free rather than to live under tyranny. But seen in this light, merely having access to the ballot, while crucial, is insufficient. Women of all kinds must participate robustly in democratic self-government and on equal footing with men. By *participate* I mean voting; I mean engaging in public deliberation through which political questions are framed, values clarified, and policy options evaluated; I mean running for legislative office and serving as lawmakers; and I mean serving in the judiciary where the law is interpreted and applied.

This suggests that a women's rights agenda must include not only efforts to ensure that all women are able to vote but also efforts to increase voter turnout and women's participation in forums for political deliberation, elective office, and the judiciary. This is a tall order as the causes of women's under-participation are complex. For example, women lack power, relative to men, in the many institutions (such as churches, universities, and think tanks) that are stepping stones to political power and influence in political debate; women have less time to dedicate to politics as they tend to carry a double burden of paid and unpaid labor; due to sex stereotyping, women, especially women of color, are often not recognized as authoritative and capable of leadership; the behavior called for in public deliberation and electoral politics is agonistic and culturally coded as masculine; and issues of special interest to women are often seen as personal and not political.

We must add that money plays an outsized role in our politics, amplifying the voices of the few wealthy, and drowning out the voices of many less advantaged. When money buys political influence, that influence is often used to solidify the advantages of wealth. Women are underrepresented among those who buy political influence. But equalizing women's share of this influence would surely be a Pyrrhic victory. The women's movement should aim instead to amplify the voices of the many less advantaged women.

We should be realistic, however, about increasing women's political participation. We have inherited our society's basic arrangements (legal and otherwise) from a past in which women of all backgrounds, the poor, and men of color had little voice. Society's basic arrangements constrain us by the sheer inertia of the way things are, but also by limiting our imaginations—limiting the kind of change we can imagine or think necessary or possible. Women—poor and otherwise, of all backgrounds—are not immune to such constraints on imagination and will. Even more disheartening is that some women's political participation is guided by racism and other exclusionary views. This is surely a limit on the benefits we may expect from increasing women's participation in politics.

Married women's legal right to own property was won gradually, state by state; New York's Married Women's Property Act (1848) was an early model (Stansell 2010). Still, after married women's legal right to own property was recognized in principle, even the most privileged women remained hindered by policies and practices that rendered women unable to manage their own financial affairs (Eveleth 2014). And the legal right to own property was no match for Jim Crow policies and practices that, all around the country and not just in the South, systematically deprived black women (and men) of the ability to accumulate wealth (Coates 2014). Related financial predation, victimizing vulnerable communities, is ongoing and contributes to the precarious economic circumstances in which millions of women (and children and men) currently find themselves (Carr 2008).

We can best understand the right to property by considering why it is worthy of struggle. The right to property is of particular interest because many assume (wrongly) that liberalism entails endorsement of laissez-faire capitalism and infer (wrongly) that the right to property promoted by liberal feminists is a right to unfettered accumulation of society's productive assets. Seen in the light of what makes the right to own property worthy of struggle, it becomes clear that the right at issue is a right to own personal property and not necessarily a right to own large portions of society's productive assets. A right to own personal property is not incompatible with versions of democratic socialism—the latter involving some sort of collective ownership of society's productive assets.

Having exclusive access to—that is, owning—personal property plays an important role in inoculating individuals against exploitation, in enabling individuals to construct lives that they value, and in being able to participate in society's shared culture as an equal. Once we appreciate this, our concern is with a whole host of policies, practices, and social arrangements that currently render millions of women (and children and men) so impoverished that they are vulnerable to exploitation, unable to participate in society's shared culture as equals, and unable to construct lives guided by their own values. Because our focus is on the role personal property plays in the status of individuals as equals in society, we are led to reject ex post remedies—like the wealth redistribution we find in our (anemic) welfare state. This is because after-the-fact redistribution from the wealthy to the poor construes the poor as unworthy recipients of the largess of a begrudged privileged class. Ex ante remedies are preferable. These are policies, practices, and institutional arrangements that ensure that such poverty does not develop in the first place (Rawls 2001, 139).

From legal measures beginning in the nineteenth century to protect women against (excessive) physical abuse by husbands, to the last state's recognition of the crime of marital rape (in 1993), to the Violence Against Women Act (1994), activists have struggled to put into law adequate recognition of women's right to be free of violence (sexual and otherwise, in the home and elsewhere) (Cooper 2003, 53–69). Despite legislative victories, women and girls continue to be subject to an alarming degree of violence and threats of violence (CDC 2017). And violence against trans women, women who are sex workers, and women who are incarcerated is at epidemic levels (Human Rights Campaign 2017; Potterat et al. 2004; Amnesty International USA 2019).

Protection of women and girls from violence and the threat of violence is worth the struggle because they can take away women's agency altogether or disempower women by reducing their sphere of activity to avoidance of harm; they also often reinforce women's subordinate role; and in the extreme, they fracture the self and reduce women's sense of their own value (Brison 2003). Seen in this light, women's right to be free of violence and the threat of violence is a crucial component of a women's rights agenda. But while more effective law enforcement must surely be a part of any remedy, we should steer clear of an overly punitive response. Rather than allowing wrongdoing to take place and then punishing wrongdoers with punitive zeal—which is our culture's wont—we should aim to change the culture so that violence against women and girls does not happen in the first place. After all, those we would punish could be our allies, our lovers, and our sons.

The right to not be steered (by moralistic and paternalistic laws) into society's preferred gender roles should be understood alongside the right to reproductive self-determination. These rights are best understood in the light of the role they play in making it possible for individuals to construct lives along the lines of their own deepest understanding of themselves and their values. These rights are as central as, and intrinsically bound up with, the rights to freedom of conscience and freedom of association and have been recognized by law. The basic principle is that the government may not enforce a "romantic paternalism," that is, a restrictive conception of women's role (Frontiero v. Richardson, 411 US 677 (1973)). The recent recognition of the right of gay men and lesbians to serve in the military, and of the right to marry a person of the same sex, is arguably an extension of that basic principle. But we have yet to see—and we should advocate for—the realization of its full implications in law and in the culture for gay men and lesbians as well as for trans women and men.

Women have a limited legal right to decide whether to carry a pregnancy to term (Roe v. Wade, 410 US 113 (1973)). But many girls and women cannot effectively exercise this right in some states due to legal hurdles that seriously encumber abortion providers (Planned Parenthood 2017). Moreover, some states have only one abortion provider (Kenning 2017). Some conservatives are working actively to ensure that the Supreme Court reverse itself on abortion. Should they be successful, women in New York would probably retain the right to reproductive self-determination, but the right is less secure in many other states. A robust agenda going forward not only must focus on protecting the limited constitutional right to an abortion that women currently enjoy but must include a larger focus on securing for women (and girls) the full array of conditions necessary for procreative self-determination.

Finally, women's right to equal educational and occupational opportunity is recognized by law but enforcement remains a problem. Our profoundly segregated public educational system effectively deprives millions of girls of the opportunity, equal to that of their more privileged peers, to develop their talents (Brown 2016). And a quick look at the media at the time of this writing indicates that women of all backgrounds continue to face sexual harassment on the job. Without the right to equality of opportunity in education and the workplace, women cannot hope to fully develop their talents and contribute to society's shared culture on an equal footing with men. This way of understanding the right to equality of opportunity focuses attention on the many common practices and attitudes that impede women's professional trajectories, such as the socializing of girls into disadvantaging and subordinating social roles, sexist and racist schemas and implicit bias, and opportunity-hoarding among men and whites. These practices and attitudes affect women of color more dramatically than white women as the former face a double burden of sex and race disadvantage.

Appreciating women's rights in the light of the purposes they serve suggests a rich and broad women's rights agenda with emphases on increasing the participation of women of all backgrounds in democratic self-governance, remedying the poverty that afflicts millions of women, changing the culture to protect all women and girls against violence, securing the conditions for reproductive and gender self-determination, and bringing an end to practices and attitudes that undermine the opportunities of women and girls of all backgrounds.

The Demand for Fairness

Many associate liberal feminism with a women's rights agenda, like the one outlined above. I argue in this section that only by supplementing a women's rights agenda with a demand for fairness would we have an adequate liberal feminist agenda for the women's movement going forward. The demand for fairness says the following: individuals must enjoy their fair share of the benefits, and shoulder their fair share of the burdens, of social life; that is, society must not be a scheme rigged to benefit some at the expense of others—either a scheme rigged to benefit men at the expense of women or one rigged to benefit some women at the expense of other women. I focus here on unfairness in how our society distributes the burden of providing caregiving for those among us who cannot care for themselves.[5]

To develop this point, I begin by calling attention to New Yorker Elizabeth Cady Stanton's address to the National American Woman Suffrage Association upon her resignation from its presidency in 1892, after serving for decades in leadership positions in the suffrage movement.[6] In the address, "The Solitude of Self," Stanton (1892) explains why the women's movement should pursue a women's rights agenda. Stanton explains that to be a fully developed individual—which is a woman's "birthright"—is to be "a solitary voyager," someone who is ultimately self-sufficient. But, Stanton tells us, such status is not possible for a woman unless she enjoys the "self-sovereignty" that rights ensure (2).

Invoking the Daniel Defoe novel, Stanton asks us to imagine the self-sovereign woman, the woman protected by rights (the "solitary voyager"), as "an imaginary Robinson Crusoe." And then she mentions Friday:

> In discussing the rights of woman, we are to consider, first,
> what belongs to her as an individual, in a world of her
> own, the arbiter of her own destiny, an imaginary Robinson
> Crusoe, with her woman, Friday, on a solitary island (1).

The original Friday, we recall, is an indigenous man, a person of color, who, in the Defoe novel, becomes Crusoe's servant. It seems that for Stanton, to have a "world of her own," to be "the arbiter of her own destiny," a woman must have "her woman, Friday" (1). She must have a servant.

Stanton was in favor of a woman's right to her own income, so perhaps the idea is that her woman Friday would be protected by rights, would earn a wage, and would be a fully developed individual herself. But the passage clearly suggests that it is necessary to have a servant to see to the home and the bodily needs of family members (especially of family members whose need for care is critical, like children and individuals with severe disabilities). I presume, though, that Friday has no such servant. (I am reminded of an undergraduate student who, in response to Mary Romero's (1997) excellent paper "Who Takes Care of the Maid's Children?," exclaimed that where she's from everyone has a maid, and was visibly flustered when I then asked whether, where she's from, the maids also have maids!)

If this is right, then Stanton is making a mistake in her address; she is conflating self-sovereignty with self-sufficiency. Self-sovereignty, or as I prefer to call it, autonomy, is what rights protect. As we have seen, in my understanding, rights provide a variety of goods: they protect one's status as coauthor of society's basic arrangements; they protect individuals against exploitation; and they enable individuals to live as they choose and to participate in society's shared culture as equals. Self-sufficiency is something different; it is not needing support, financial or otherwise.

Autonomy does not entail self-sufficiency conceptually; we can imagine an autonomous person who is not self-sufficient. But in the real world, social arrangements can make being self-sufficient a condition for being autonomous, that is, for enjoying the goods rights protect. One way that social arrangements can do this is by allowing caregiving obligations that render individuals dependent on others for support (financial and otherwise) to disqualify individuals from enjoying all or some of the goods rights protect. That is what social arrangements did in Stanton's day; the social role of those who provided care was that of servant or subservient wife. Hence the lure of the conflation. Oddly, Stanton and others who have touted the ideal of self-sufficiency fail to recognize the dependency of the purported self-sufficient individual on the labor of others. Surely the truth is, as Eva Kittay (1999) has asserted, that society is a system of nested dependencies, not an aggregate of self-sufficient individuals.

Unfortunately, social arrangements that make being self-sufficient (or at least being able to command the services of a wife or a servant) a condition for being autonomous are not merely a thing of the past. Our society's current basic arrangements pit providing care for one's dependents against enjoying many of the goods that make rights worth the struggle. This disadvantage is experienced most dramatically by women, but the brunt of it is felt by women who can't afford to off-load their caregiving obligations to other people; in our society that is poor women.

In the United States today, providing care to dependents frustrates caregivers' ability to develop their talents and compete for positions that confer social recognition and authority, and frustrates their ability to earn income, accumulate wealth, and access time away from paid work necessary for activities that define a good life for them. In families with a heterosexual couple at its heart, women still do most of the work of caring for the home and for dependents (Kranz-Kent 2009, 46–59). The common refrain that men should help out misses its target when we note that many millions of women are raising children, and caring for aging and disabled family members, without a resident male partner. But even when there is a resident male adult, he too is bound by the rules of conventional educational institutions and workplaces, which assume that the employee has no dependency obligations. That is, exhorting men to take up 50 percent of work in the home won't alleviate dependency-related disadvantage; it will only spread the disadvantage around more evenly among adults in a family.

Affluent families can avoid much of this disadvantage by outsourcing caregiving work to others for pay. The surfeit of women willing to do this work—often immigrants and women of color, under conditions that include long hours, low pay, no health insurance, and no paid days off—is a boon to affluent women and their families. When poor women take care of affluent women's dependents and homes, affluent women are freed up to pursue enriching work outside the home. This also frees affluent women to volunteer and otherwise nurture the larger associations that allow their communities to thrive. Poor women can rarely pass their domestic work on to someone else; they rarely escape the disadvantage and often pass it on to their communities.

Those who can afford to off-load caregiving work to others for pay (or support a family caregiver at home) can "lean in" at work (Sandberg 2013)—as many exhort women to do—while also seeing to it that their dependents receive the care they need. The many who can't afford to off-load caregiving work to others often find themselves nonetheless required to "lean in" at work outside of the home, leaving them unable to provide the kind of nurturing their dependents and communities need. Thus, we have groups with unequal abilities to provide care to their dependents and groups whose need for caregiving is unequally satisfied. These inequalities are not trivial. There are serious care deficits in communities whereby many cannot afford to provide or procure the kind of care their dependents need, and such deficits contribute to the intergenerational transfer of poverty and disadvantage.

The dominant ethos in the United States celebrates self-sufficiency. This means recognizing caregiving needs, if at all, as private—that is, as the sole responsibility of individuals—and delegates their satisfaction to women and girls by socializing them to the discrete social role of caregiver (and disadvantaging them for it). This ethos celebrates families and communities that satisfy their dependency needs privately; it conceives of their dependents as worthy of care and their women as virtuous for providing it. The flip side of this ethos is the stigmatizing and blaming of families and communities that are rendered, by social arrangements, unable to satisfy their caregiving needs privately; for example, dependents in such families are construed as unworthy of receiving, and caregivers as unworthy of providing or procuring needed care. Just as pervasive is a racist ethos stigmatizing black and brown caregiving—a refusal to recognize black and brown people as worthy of receiving care, and black and brown caregivers as entitled to provide or procure care for their dependents. It is impossible to disentangle the classist from the racist (and especially antiblack) aspects of this ethos, but it is equally clear that the latter is not reducible to the former. When confronted with the fact that the affluent are praised for keeping a parent at home to care for children while the poor are told to work and leave their children in substandard childcare arrangements, some offer veiled racism in response. The thought seems to be that affluent women are virtuous and use their freedom from paid work to benefit their children, while poor women—read "black women"—are lazy and undeserving and will abuse welfare state benefits.

Every society has caregiving needs. All of us are born and remain for nearly two decades dependent on the caregiving of others, and many of us become dependent on caregiving later in life. What's more, those who provide care for others often themselves become dependent on others for support, including income, because often providing needed care is incompatible with remunerative work. This is simply the way things are. This is what Eva Kittay (1999) calls "the fact of dependency." The question is only, How is the burden of providing care, and the benefit of receiving it, to be distributed? What does justice require? My answer is that justice requires that it be distributed fairly. Society must not be a scheme rigged to benefit some at the expense of others; individuals must enjoy their fair share of the benefits and shoulder their fair share of the burdens of social life, and that includes the burdens and benefits of caregiving.

Conclusion

I have argued that while a women's rights agenda—including the right to vote celebrated in this volume—is crucial, it has not been fully achieved. I showed that this is especially clear when we appreciate why women's legal rights are worthy of struggle. However, I have also argued that a women's right agenda, even the relatively rich one I presented, must be supplemented by a demand for fairness in the distribution of caregiving. A focus on fairness in this area calls for changes in how we organize caregiving work in our society, changes in our workplaces and educational institutions, and much more. This fairness agenda does not call for redistributive policies which allow unfairness to accumulate and then take from the rich and give to the poor. Such policies leave the offending institutional structures in place, structures that construe the rich as entitled to feeling begrudged and the poor as undeserving and humiliated. A focus on fairness in caregiving calls for ex ante measures that ensure an unfair distribution of the benefits and burdens of caregiving doesn't arise in the first place.

It is particularly important to note that focusing on a fair distribution of caregiving keeps our eye on Stanton's Friday, that is, on the lived experience and needs and interests of women, but especially of women who currently carry a disproportionate share of society's caregiving burdens. It also keeps our eye on those who are in need of care to survive and thrive; this is, of course, each one of us when we are young, severely disabled, or infirm in old age. Such a focus is particularly apt as we move into yet another century of feminist political activism in New York and elsewhere.

Notes

1. Thanks are due to Jasmine Syedullah for helpful comments on an earlier version of this draft.
2. For an excellent overview of the first and second waves of the US women's movement, see Stansell (2010).
3. This way of putting the demand for fairness is due to Rawls (1971).
4. Felon disenfranchisement must be counted as suppression of the black vote. For more, see Wood et al. (2009).
5. Performing caregiving work can be profoundly enriching, but this fact does not warrant disadvantaging those who perform it.
6. The address was delivered that same year also to the Committee of the Judiciary of the United States Congress.

Works Cited

Amnesty International USA. 2019. "Women in Custody." Accessed October 17, 2019. https://www.amnestyusa.org/pdf/custodyissues.pdf.

Berman, Ari. 2016. "There Are 868 Fewer Places to Vote in 2016 Because the Supreme Court Gutted the Voting Rights Act." *Nation*, November 4, 2016. https://www.thenation.com/article/there-are-868-fewer-places-to-vote-in-2016-because-the-supreme-court-gutted-the-voting-rights-act/.

Brison, Susan. 2003. *Aftermath: Violence and the Remaking of a Self*. Princeton, NJ: Princeton University Press.

Brown, Emma. 2016. "On the Anniversary of Brown v. Board, New Evidence That U.S. Schools Are Resegregating." *Washington Post*, May 17, 2016. https://www.washingtonpost.com/news/education/wp/2016/05/17/on-the-anniversary-of-brown-v-board-new-evidence-that-u-s-schools-are-resegregating/.

Carr, James H. 2008. *Segregation: The Rising Costs for America.* New York: Routledge.

Coates, Ta-Nehisi. 2014. "The Case for Reparations." *Atlantic*, June 2014. https://www.theatlantic.com/magazine/archive/2014/06/the-case-for-reparations/361631/.

Davis, Peggy Cooper. 2003. "Women, Bondage, and the Reconstructed Constitution." In *Women and the Constitution: History, Interpretation, and Practice*, edited by Sibyl A. Schwarzenbach and Patricia Smith, 53–69. New York: Columbia University Press.

Eveleth, Rose. 2014. "Forty Years Ago, Women Had a Hard Time Getting Credit Cards." *Smithsonian*, January 8, 2014. https://www.smithsonianmag.com/smart-news/forty-years-ago-women-had-a-hard-time-getting-credit-cards-180949289/.

Human Rights Campaign. 2017. *A Time to Act: Fatal Violence Against Transgender People in America in 2017.* https://assets2.hrc.org/files/assets/resources/A_Time_To_Act_2017_REV3.pdf.

Kenning, Chris. 2017. "Kentucky Trial Could Make State First in U.S. With No Abortion Clinic." Reuters, September 6, 2017. https://www.reuters.com/article/us-kentucky-abortion/kentucky-trial-could-make-state-first-in-u-s-with-no-abortion-clinic-idUSKCN1BH17P.

Kittay, Eva. 1999. *Love's Labor: Essays on Women, Equality, and Dependency.* New York: Routledge.

Kranz-Kent, Rachel. 2009 "Measuring Time Spent in Unpaid Household Work: Results from the American Time Use Survey." *Monthly Labor Review* 132, no. 7 (July): 46–59.

Planned Parenthood. 2017. "Federal and State Bans and Restrictions on Abortion." Accessed December 31, 2017. https://www.plannedparenthoodaction.org/issues/abortion/federal-and-state-bans-and-restrictions-abortion.

Potterat, John J., Devon D. Brewer, Stephen Q. Muth, Richard B. Rothenberg, Donald E. Woodhouse, John B. Muth, Heather K. Stites, and Brody Stuart. 2004. "Mortality in a Long-Term Open Cohort of Prostitute Women." *American Journal of Epidemiology* 159 (8): 778–85.

Rawls, John. 1971. *A Theory of Justice.* Cambridge, MA: Harvard University Press.

Rawls, John. 2001. *Justice as Fairness: A Restatement.* Cambridge, MA: Harvard University Press.

Roediger, David. 2008. *How Race Survived U.S. History.* New York: Verso.

Romero, Mary. 1997. "Who Takes Care of the Maid's Children? Exploring the Costs of Domestic Service. In *Feminism and Families*, edited by Hilde Lindeman, 63–91. New York: Routledge.

Sandberg, Sheryl. 2013. *Lean In: Women, Work, and the Will to Lead.* New York: Alfred A. Knopf.

Stansell, Christine. 2010. *The Feminist Promise*. New York: Random House.

Stanton, Elizabeth Cady. 1892. *Solitude of Self: Address Delivered by Mrs. Stanton before the Committee of the Judiciary of the United States Congress, Monday, January 18, 1892*. Library of Congress. https://www.loc.gov/resource/rbnawsa.n8358/?st=gallery.

Wood, Erika, Liz Budnitz, Garima Malhotra, and Charles Ogletree. 2009. *Jim Crow in New York*. The Brennan Center. https://www.brennancenter.org/sites/default/files/2019-08/Report_JIMCROWNY_2010.pdf.

Chapter 8

Making Freedom Moves

The Abolitionist Praxis of Black Women's Liberation

JASMINE SYEDULLAH AND GABRIELLE BARON-HILL

"Of the many contributions that feminist theories make to our strategies," Professor Angela Davis reminded her audience in a recent public lecture, is that "it is often the case that the greatest and most productive insights emanate from what appears to be the smallest and most marginal problem" (Davis 2013).

We open this reflection on the role of black women in the work of suffrage movements with Davis's quote because her provocation turns our attention straightaway to the significance and contestation surrounding the merit of those living in the margins, and raises questions about the value of their insights into our most pressing social problems. It also suggests that our national understanding of the limits of suffrage for black liberation raises concerns for commonsense understandings of liberal political rights discourse. As Rosalyn Terborg-Penn (1999, 10) writes, "The right to vote is a privilege only recently exercised by the majority of African American women in the United States." The question that drives this essay asks, Was voting ever going to be strong enough a strategy to realize the political possibilities implied in black women's victories over the dispossessions of disenfranchisement, however provisional, forgotten, or unseen?

At the time, Davis was speaking about the relatively small population of incarcerated women in US prisons.[1] Though their numbers are small, Davis argued that women in prison were in possession of a distinctly gendered perspective on the problem of mass incarceration, its effects, and its ability to undermine the sovereignty and self-determination of black communities. As a black feminist whose own strength of vision and insight came both by way of rigorous study and by way of surviving FBI scrutiny, suspicion, and criminalization, Davis reminds her audience that what she brings to feminist theory is not an anomaly, and she does not travel alone. There are many would-be feminists as yet unknown to the struggle for women's rights, those whose efforts are systemically sidelined by the movements they advance, voices silenced multiple times over, by their era, by history. Because there are so many whose testimonies are wholly absent from our disciplined understandings and very best analyses of the major social problems and obstacles to social change that define the so-called American "experiment," much work remains to be done to recover their stories, bear witness to the wrongs they write, and set their visions for liberation alongside national narratives of freedom in an effort to better understand how far they would say we have come.[2]

Many of those would-be feminist theorists who have long been made to move along the margins, made to strategize for their self-defense without the protections of the law, were asked to wait their turn while sacrificing much to support liberation movements from the backstage. Many of those who struggled to sustain the movement for rights and equality under the heightened scrutiny, suspicion, and criminalization of the hostile territories they called home are not often celebrated as central figures in historical accounts of the social transformations that movements for social justice helped to shape. Before the formal emergence of black women to party politics in New York City with the state-centered activism of Anna Arnold Hedgeman, Dorothy Height, Eunice Hunton Carter, and Pauli Murray, women worked together after the Civil War to build communities, resources, and networks to support black lives through the formation of women's clubs.[3] In her essay "Mary Church Terrell and the National Association of Colored Women, 1896 to 1901," Beverly W. Jones (1982, 21) writes on the social contexts out of which these reformist communities emerged. Jones makes the point that the

> proliferation of black women's clubs . . . owed their genesis
> to the peculiar circumstances of black life in general and spe-
> cifically to discrimination against black women . . . Fannie

Barrier Williams, a noted black club woman and activist, later recalled that "the club movement among colored women had grown out of the organized anxiety of women who have only recently become intelligent enough to recognize their social condition and strong enough to initiate and apply the forces of reform."

With limited access to claims of respectability, never mind personhood, many black women not only formed their own activist spaces but were navigating a politics of visibility whose terrain was only evidenced by their refusal to be domesticated by politics as usual. They were made, by their conditions, to reimagine the possibilities of political action beyond their personal investments in self-preservation, their family's safety, or community well-being. Their "organized anxieties" seeded desires for justice to hold their collectives to account for the innumerable uncontainable injuries of slavery. What began as decentralized networks of resistance during slavery reemerged after the Civil War as the unconventional formalization of bondspeople's protocols of political power from the plantation. Their contested disruptions of the white supremacist patriarchal order of public protest refused the geographies of containment that kept black women from moving, as Stephanie Camp's (2004) work reminds us, "closer to freedom," even after the end of slavery.

Though black men and women have been fighting for the vote since before the end of slavery, their place in the national accounting for these histories is rarely well represented. Stephanie Camp's historical account of women fighting for their freedom from slavery provides numerous examples of the kinds of everyday ways black women moved "closer to freedom" long before the shackles fell from the plantation South. Susan Goodier writes about the work of black women activists living in New York State to establish groups such as the Colored Woman's Suffrage League of Brooklyn, founded by Sarah J.S. Tompkins Garnet. Goodier (2017, 478) writes, "for many black women who worked for their enfranchisement, gaining woman suffrage represented only one aspect of their activist agendas. For example, most black women's organizations supported the Harriet Tubman home for old folks in Auburn, settlement houses, and the Frederick Douglass memorial in Rochester, regularly contributing money members had raised."

Though a few commemorated black women's contributions to the abolitionist movement and the struggles for political incorporation after slavery, the rise of black feminist communities in the late twentieth century brought renewed attention to these hidden histories, particularly the intersectional role of black women in advancing the conditions of black communities from the era of emancipation to the rise of the civil rights movement. Angela Davis (1972, 86) wrote from prison in 1971 of black women's resistance to the dehumanizing effects of slavery's hold on the community of enslaved people as, "an organic ingredient of slave life." She highlights the ways black women's resistance was rooted in the ways they cared for themselves and their families even after working in the fields and in the domestic spaces they could not own. From the plantations, to the fugitive routes to freedom, to the formation of antislavery societies and women's clubs in the North, nineteenth-century black women were the would-be feminists of their communities. They worked at the intersections of the free labor movement, the antislavery movement, and the early movement for women's liberation. Their contributions to stories of political progress do not follow neat linear trajectories of ascent from margin to center, or from chattel to citizen.

Many have been made to move along the margins of political life as a standard practice of resistance to the systemic alienation of the misogynist, heteronormative, white-supremacist, settler-colonial gaze of national belonging. Some worked the edges of their situated knowledges of power by exercising an appearance of deference to those with dominion over the sacred arena of public civic life—bowing to their master's gods, ideals, and aesthetics is often a necessary evil to suffer for the right to gain entry. Marked as they were by multiple intersections of structural discrimination, their voices, witness, and testimony were routinely displaced, time and again, from the very entitlements and protections their contributions to political progress helped to manifest. Despite their unconscionable depredations, violent dispossessions, and inhumane proximity to premature death, as geographer Ruth Gilmore (2007) would remind us, those living in the margins of our modern society are not without power. Their chronic displacement to the wasted spaces of western expansion requires an ever-expanding migration of perspective, sharpened, by necessity, by an ability to see what is most often rendered invisible. Moving along the margins of the political has long meant knowing how to wait for the right time to move to action. Moving along the margins of the political meant no one might know how to save you as well as you do, that waiting for salvation from the dangers of being seen, seeking protections from the intimate, vigilante, or state-sanctioned harm that met women on the way to work, in the home, and in the midst of their attempts to defend themselves and their families, could prove fatal or worse.[4]

For many women, another embodiment of politics was necessary, a political practice passed down by means of the kinds of deep intelligence gathering that Davis and bell hooks and the Combahee River Collective would eventually codify as black feminism. It is an ancestral political practice passed down to remember that which resisted being seen. We are moving histories of black women's contributions to national political life from the margins of nineteenth- and twentieth-century social movements to the center of our organizing for black life today. It is a black feminist political practice of social change that had its origins in the earliest beginnings of women's movements for liberation, suffrage, equal rights, and protections. It is a political practice that proclaimed, "No one will speak for us but ourselves" (Gordon 1972, 2). It was a politics that recognized that many white women saw their need for the right to vote along a different trajectory than that of black women. While white women wanted to be freed from having to live under the "thumb" of their white male counterparts, black women saw political participation as both a means to free themselves from "physical and spiritual" bondage of the multiple patriarchal institutions that held them hostage and a way to ensure the freedom of black children and communities not yet born.[5]

The reconstitution of black women's contributions to the national formation of political life brought about by the interventions of black feminists to both women's liberation movements and black liberation movements in the late twentieth century reordered conventional understandings of the progress narrative passed down since the end of slavery. Though long marginalized, black women's contributions to the framing of our national consciousness of freedom has played a prophetic role in the formation of these movements along the margins, against the injustices of "law and order" politics. Moving along the margins meant both that they received little recognition for the landmark contributions they have made to mainstream politics and that the marks they left were rarely indistinguishable from their more readily legible counterparts, those of white women and black men.

One is reminded of the black feminist theory of *But Some of Us Are Brave* and Barbara Smith's (1979, 48) definition of feminism as "the political theory and practice that struggles to free all women: women of color, working-class women, poor women, disabled women, lesbians, old women—as well as white, economically privileged, heterosexual women. Anything less than this vision of total freedom is not feminism, but merely female self-aggrandizement." The expansive intersectional trajectories of black feminists' distinctly raced and gendered perspectives on social movement strategy and ideology that continue to escape recognition even today have their roots in histories of erasure that have concealed black women's contributions to American politics within narratives of national progress.[6] More than an identity politics, then, intersectionality is strategy for inhabiting overlapping structures of oppression in unusual ways. As late nineteenth-century social activist S. Elizabeth Frazier referred to them in an 1892 talk before the Brooklyn Literary Union, the deeds and testaments of "African American women of mark" are representative of a small but powerful community working within the early women's rights movement, some of whom were moving toward a kind of freedom even freeborn men could not have easily imagined.

More than fifteen years before the Women's Rights Committee convened in Seneca Falls, Maria W. Stewart (2010) addressed the Boston public on the "cause of freedom." As early as 1837, black women were organizing for their personal sovereignty and freedom from the paternalism of the law. "Though a few individuals had advanced the notion of a woman's right to vote . . . women at the meeting," writes historian Ann D. Gordon, "defined politics more loosely as the right to be heard." Gordon (1997, 3–4) quotes their resolve at length, noting "that it is the duty of woman, and the province of woman, to plead the cause of the oppressed in our land, and to do all that she can by her voice, and her pen, and her purse, and the influence of her example, to overthrow the horrible system of slavery."

The antislavery movement's role in the formation of suffragist societies and their imaginations of political liberation made for a complex and overlapping matrix of political communities throughout what they so aptly referred to as the "nominally Free States" of the antebellum North. More than the vote, then, moving along the margins of political progress became for black women generative of a keen kind of orientation toward a project of liberation that exceeded the colorblind oracle of a law that legitimized chattel slavery, a vision that required more than legal recognition and inclusion, but, of necessity, the wholesale abolition of the prejudice that preserved the institute of slavery, a prejudice that would not be abolished with the constitutional end of the patriarchal institution or overcome with the eventual enfranchisement of women. Beyond suffrage, black women's liberation movements mobilized in service to the black men, children, and women, and the people who remained at risk of being returned to captivity precisely because of the exception clause written into the constitutional abolition of slavery in the Thirteenth Amendment, which states, "Neither slavery nor involuntary servitude, except as a punishment for crime whereof the party shall have been duly convicted, shall exist within the United States, or any place subject to their jurisdiction."

"While the chains of slavery had been broken," Angela Davis (2011, 77) writes in her *Women, Race, and Class*, "black people still suffered the pain of economic deprivation and they faced the terrorist violence of racist mobs in a form whose intensity was unmatched even by slavery." The promises of sisterhood and cross-racial solidarity that stemmed from the intersections of the early women's liberation movements and the movement against slavery were ultimately insufficient to prevent black women's erasure from the concerns of the white members of their "sisterhood." Black women had too long suffered abuse and indifference from white women. Black women who were serious about fighting for their right to vote knew they would also need to fight for the right to be seen as citizens worthy of the law's protection. They would have to organize for their defense from the injustice of the law itself. Suffrage alone would be insufficient. The abolition of slavery would not be enough.

Alchemy of Erasure[7]

Since freedom from the domestic violence of national belonging would not be won with the vote, the precarious claims to freedom that formerly enslaved black women could count on were fundamentally different from the kinds of freedom either white women or black men could hope to win, either in the time of slavery or in the wake of its constitutional abolition. As Sarah Haley (2016, 87) writes in her book *No Mercy Here*, "They [black women] were situated in opposition to normative femininity. They were situated in opposition to the normative gender position, and produced outside of binary oppositional gender categories as something else altogether; that 'else' was contradictory and ambiguous."

Though black women's positions in the domestic order of the nation were without the distinctions of gender granted their white counterparts, white women often used the subjection of black women that slavery sanctioned to lay claim to their own place of provisional proximity to power within the province of the law's paternalistic domestication of all who lived within its bounds. Victoria Woodhull was the first white women to use the phrase "sexual slavery" to critique the gender violence of the institution of marriage. Elizabeth Cady Stanton compared the denial of her right to refuse her husband her body according to the bonds of marriage to the sexual subjection of black women under chattel slavery. Though the elision of the two injuries erases the hierarchies of power and proximity to harm that link both, Stanton's subsuming of black women's plight in the lived experience of her own struggles for sexual sovereignty suggests that the kinds of freedom black women were fighting for could not easily be understood as something distinct from, or other than, the kinds of freedom white women could imagine for themselves. Because they were, as Haley (2016, 87) notes, "situated in opposition to the normative gender position," their position could be readily instrumentalized toward the ends of those whose gender positions were perceived as more readily normative, familiar, and unambiguous.[8]

The question we must ask, then, is whose struggles for freedom challenge the meaning of freedom won by the passage of the Nineteenth Amendment and for whom were the limits of suffrage visible long before its demand was made law, and why. It is far too easy to suggest, not to mention inaccurate to suppose, that in order to see the limits of the law's protections one would need to see freedom from the displaced position of a black woman. White women were also wise to the limits of suffrage and contributed in great numbers to the cause of abolition. However, because it was the tendency of early feminists to subsume others' lived experiences of gender violence and political exclusion as their own, distinguishing between the political vision of white women suffragists and the formerly enslaved black women who worked both for them and with them for the vote remains difficult to discern.

As part of the ongoing efforts to disentangle the intersections of feminist history forged out of the struggle to end slavery, historians gathered at the University of Massachusetts in the late 1980s to piece together the story of the race relations of the woman suffrage movement. Elsa Barkley Brown, Bettina Aptheker, John Bracey, Evelyn Brooks Higginbotham, and others who had convened eventually decided to organize their conference around the guiding question, "What is the political history of black women?" (Gordon and Collier-Thomas 1997, 7). What did the black women of the "nominally Free States" refuse to give up in their coalition with white women's liberation? What does it mean for them to be constantly displaced within the movement, but be called on to represent its cause in both theory and practice? The domestic politics of everyday life for black women working for the "cause of liberation" was a labor of love that left many with no place of their own in the movements for their own liberation. The devaluation of their contributions by their contemporaries cannot be redeemed by our recuperation of that history; however, it is in our commitment to try to discern what, to black women, freedom might have meant by turning attention to the clubs they convened and national conferences they created out of this tension. As Josephine Pierre Ruffin, president of the Women's Era Club, shared at the First National Conference of the Colored Women of America in 1895, "white women have protested against the admission of colored women into any organization on the ground of the immorality of our women. . . . It is 'most right,' and our boundless duty to stand forth and declare ourselves and principles to teach an ignorant and suspicious world that our aims and interests are identical with those of aspiring women" (Jones 1982, 23).

What might we, as the generational inheritors of their steady declarations, do to better honor their efforts as the conditions of possibility for our own ability to move along the margins of politics and power, and to shape the routes of survival that remain within regimes of US domestic authority, conditions that continue to bend women, men, and trans and gender non-conforming people from variously marginalized corners of its domain to its will, generation after generation. It is for this reason that a study of black women's continuation of the work of liberation movements is more than a merely identitarian side project marginal to the study of "real" politics or feminist history. Indeed, it is research that understands that the greatest obstacle to the realization of the democratic dream of equality under the law is not ideological but economic. It is an approach to the study of politics that understands that the limits of suffrage are found in the unfinished work of abolition.

The Abolitionist Origins of Women's Liberation

In 1840, Angelina and Sarah Grimke spoke out publicly against slavery, attracting audiences of women only but then increasing their reach to attract men. Clergy took issue with their rise in visibility and actively sought to deprive women of the right to vote in business meetings throughout the early antislavery conventions. Their instigating dissent of the women's leadership gave rise to a division at the annual meeting of the Anti-Slavery Association in 1840. That same year, in London, at the World Anti-Slavery Convention, abolitionists sent a call out to all the societies. White women abolitionists were sent from American societies to represent the cause. "After going three thousand miles to attend a World's convention, it was discerned that women formed no part of the constituent elements of the moral world. In summoning the friends of the slave from all parts of the hemispheres to meet in London, John Bull never dreamed that women, too, would answer to his call" (Stanton et al. 1985, 61). The women were promptly voted out of the convention, and despite incredible arguments made in support of their contributions to it, the convention delegates voted overwhelmingly for their exclusion. "As Lucretia Mott and Elizabeth Cady Stanton wended their way arm and arm down the great queen street that night . . . they agreed to hold a women's rights convention on their return to America, as the men whom they had just listened had manifested great need of some education on that question" (Stanton et al. 1985, 61).

Though support for abolition brought women together across lines of race following the historic meeting at Seneca Falls in 1848 for a convention to "discuss the social, civil, and religious condition and rights of women" (Stanton et al., 1985, 67), between 1865 and 1885, the early women's movement split over support for the Fourteenth and Fifteenth Amendments. Though the Fourteenth made citizens of the formerly enslaved and the Fifteenth gave them the vote, the latter's language failed to extend the franchise to include women. The women's movement split into two groups, the National Woman Suffrage Association (NWSA) and the American Woman Suffrage Association (AWSA). The AWSA supported the amendment for "negro suffrage," while the NWSA aggressively fought it in favor of an all-or-none politics of the franchise. While a few black women, Sojourner Truth among them, chose to back universal suffrage over the passage of "negro suffrage," most saw the urgency of supporting the passage of the Fifteenth Amendment as a priority, fearing its loss could forever foreclose the possibility of extending the right of the formerly enslaved to vote. As historian Rosalyn Terborg-Penn (1999, 9) writes, "This era is important for the development of black women's clubs . . . . Since emancipation, more and more Black women had become educated and were working to uplift their communities. However, throughout the nineteenth century, the majority of the nation's Black women had little opportunity to participate in organized woman suffrage activities." Val Marie Johnson's (2017) essay "The Half Has Never Been Told" centers on the activism of schoolteacher Maritcha Lyons, an African American women who cofounded one of the first women's rights and racial justice organizations in the United States, the Women's Loyal Union (WLU) of New York and Brooklyn, on December 5, 1892, with Victoria Earle Matthews as president. The WLU was recognized for its anti-lynching work in alliance with Ida B. Wells. In its report at the First National Conference of the Colored Women of America, the WLU stated, "We have for our watchwords, 'Vigilant, Patriotic, and Steadfast.' Our object is the diffusion of accurate and extensive information relative to the civil and social status of the colored American citizen, that they may be directed to an intelligent assertion of their rights, and unite in the employment of all lawful means to secure and retain the undisputed exercise of them" (National Association of Colored Women's Clubs 1978, 13).

Hidden in Plain Sight

Rather than attempting to defend or condemn the limits of white women's investments in the intersectional politics involved in the movement to end slavery because of their exclusion of black women's voices, witness, and wisdom at these crucial junctures of sisterhood and cross-racial solidarity, we need to ask what contributions, in particular, black women made to the work of liberation. How might their visions of freedom, however sidelined, have helped to shape a practice of feminist critique, not only of patriarchy, or of the wrong of slavery, but of the very meaning of liberation that white folks were "privileged" to imagine? Though it was not always and everywhere the case that black women held the most radical view of what freedom might mean, even today it is the case that for many, being black is an experience of observation and critique of that violence which others take for granted. Even in the context of the Civil War, a refrain that emerged from the refugees of the plantations who arrived in the nation's capital just as the reign of slavery was abolished within its borders asked, "Is this freedom?"

"Is this freedom?" is the unanswered question New York abolitionist and Hudson Valley author Harriet Jacobs (1987, 201) infers when she writes at the end of her 1861 slave narrative that she and her children "are as free from the power of slaveholders as are the white people of the north; and though that, according to my ideas, is not saying a great deal, it is a vast improvement in my condition." Like her and many others, without a place to call their own in the movement for black liberation, I read in Jacobs's ending a critique of the degree of freedom white people actually have gained from wielding the power of slavery in defense of their own liberation. I read her disappointment as a profoundly insightful understanding that the shackles of white supremacy keep white folks captive too! What if, Jacobs seems to suggest, what black women's contributions to the cause of liberation make visible are the kinds of freedom white supremacy make all but impossible to imagine? What if that failure of imagination were not simply cast off as a "black problem" but taken seriously as a global one?

Some of the roots of human rights demands have their origins in black women's activism. According to historian Susan Goodier, Hester Jeffrey's human rights approach exceeded the bounds of women's groups. Goodier (2017, 484) writes,

> On September 15, 1898 [Jeffrey] attended a conference
> in Rochester to revitalize the National Afro-American

League, its goal to "take up the work for the improvement of the colored race where it was left off by the death of Frederick Douglass." Joining J. W. Thompson, T. Thomas Fortune, Susan B. Anthony, Ida B. Wells Barnett, and other prominent activists, she helped restructure the National Afro-American Council from the Afro-American League. The Council stood out since very few organizations of its kind at the time welcomed women. Jeffrey served in various offices including as ninth vice president, then as sixth vice president. Many of the same individuals involved with the Council would eventually establish the National Association for the Advancement of Colored People.

If political legibility under the law makes black lives vulnerable to its violence, its exclusions, its patrols, its police, and its punishment, then what makes white folks think they will remain safe from the effects of their own self-preservation? The question Jacob's and other black women's work for liberation invites us to ask is, If this isn't the freedom we'd hoped to find in the wake of slavery, then what is this and how do we abolish it? Perhaps, they might tell us, voices hushed, that securing freedom is always and in every instance an illegal act, an illicit course of movement along the margins that requires we steal what we have never owned to lay claim to a dream most cannot yet imagine. Perhaps, as we move illicitly, they implore us to move with poetic license, and take a page from the legal piracy of those who justify the forced extraction of our power to fuel their lives and futures and proclaim, at least publicly, that our demands are just and that we are indeed acting piously and within "the employment of all lawful means to secure and retain the undisputed exercise of them." Or, perhaps, our black feminist great-grandmothers and aunties would warn us that the justice we seek, that dream of our lives, cannot truly be won by means of taking the same freedoms that justified our subjection.

To quote Andre Lorde (2015), "The absence of these considerations weakens any feminist discussion of the personal and the political." If what we want is increased life chances and what the law has to offer by way of protections from nationalist, racist, classist, sexist, homophobic, transphobic, and ableist discrimination is rights, then what we need to be able to do is *not* stop at the knowledge that the personal is political. But rather, we must work to overcome the seductions of possessive individualism and personal recognition, and even risk illegibility by making the political *social*. As Lorde (2015, 112) writes, "[T]o make common cause with those others identified as outside the structures in order to define and seek a world in which we can all flourish. It is learning how to take our differences and make them strengths. For the master's tools will never dismantle the master's house. They may allow us temporarily to beat him at his own game, but they will never enable us to bring about genuine change." What's more, these entitlements to legal protection are insufficient to realize the dreams of freedom our movements work to make reality. They can be rolled back, overruled, and redacted, even lost from our collective consciousness unless there is a collectively held record, testimonies not only of our formal legal victories, but also of the illicit protocols of our struggle we used to get there. Without them, the liberties of legibility, the credibility of the respectability will comfort us until we forget to remember how we got free, how we had to become fugitive before we were fighting, how we had to break the rules even as we hoped to be protected by them, how we had to become criminal before we could be credible.

In conclusion, the vote was more than political, more than freedom of choice. It gave black women the legal right to fight for their lives and the lives of their communities. It gave them the freedom to defend their legal ownership of their own bodies. The ability to fight for the kinds of life chances black women imagine for themselves today through movements for black lives has been made possible by black women's contributions to movements for liberation in the nineteenth century. They sacrificed their bodies, energy, and time so that more members of the next generation could read and write and vote. They were fighting against slavery, sexual assault, poverty, and unemployment, all for a better quality of life for their families and their family's families—for our families! As New York City black suffragist Grace P. Campbell (1925) writes in her account of the criminalization of black women,

> the number of colored women and girls convicted of proposition, Violation of the Tenement House Law, etc., is relatively larger than white; but when it is considered that the colored woman, and especially young colored girls, are the least protected group, this can be understood. There

are fewer protective homes for them before they fall. No woman's hotel or public lodging places under social supervision where the lone girl or woman may live at a moderate rate . . . The average colored woman's wage is less than that of the white: there is but small or no margin to cover periods of unemployment or sickness. While the economic problem cannot be looked upon as the sole factor in the question of prostitution among colored girls, or indeed any girls, yet it must be faced as a prime factor in their fall. Especially is this true when the standard and cost of living is understood and duly considered. Moreover, even the most law abiding citizens who look closely into the matter of arrests among colored women must admit that many are unwarranted . . . The practice of giving short sentences in the workhouse to young colored girls is undoubtedly the cause of the high percentage of colored women in that institution. The degradation of putting unfortunate young colored women in the work-house with hardened offenders can hardly be over-estimated. The loss of self-respect and vice learned by them are appalling.

The court-watching activism of black women like Grace Campbell no doubt laid the groundwork that made the rise of abolitionist efforts of leaders like Angela Davis imaginable. The critical contributions of black women's vision of justice transformed what activism looked like in the early women's rights movement despite having been and continuing to be marginalized. Black women's works are generally read as complementary to their black male contemporaries in the abolitionist movements as well as to their sisters in the women's rights movement. However, upon a closer reading, what becomes clear is that, from the start, the vision and practices of freedom that black women manifested in their struggles for waged labor, abolition, and the vote detail a distinct and far less binary understanding of the kind of freedom that comes after slavery. Our commitment is to sit with them, to learn from their witness and imagine what freedom might look like to future generations of black women. How do we build foundations that they can build upon? How we wield our power now can ensure we pass on the kinds of strength needed to survive the erasures, violence, and suspicion of national belonging to come. What we are learning is that freedom is not a right, but a steady practice of collective movement, and it is once again time to get in formation.

Notes

1. According to Federal Bureau of Prisons statistics, updated February 24, 2018, women made up only 6.8 percent of the US prison population, amounting to just over 12,500 incarcerated women. Though their numbers are small, a 2016 report by the Vera Institute of Justice and the John D. and Catherine T. MacArthur Foundation's Safety and Justice Challenge program revealed that rates of incarcerated women around the world, many of them black and brown, are the fastest rising of any prison demographic.

2. As Susan Goodier (2017, 477) writes in her essay "Historian's Corner: Seeking and Seeing Black Women: Hester C. Jeffrey and Woman Suffrage Activism," "The greatest boon for revealing black women's social and political activism is, of course, the Internet. Increasingly, rare books, pamphlets, and other documents are being scanned and made widely accessible. Virtually all sizable cities in New York had at least one African American newspaper, although many of those that are extant remain to be scanned and made available online. We need to demand that these resources be made widely available."

3. For more on black women's activism and political participation in New York City politics, see Julie A. Gallagher's *Black Women and Politics in New York City* (University of Illinois Press, 2012).

4. For a detailed and exquisitely penned history of black women's subjection after the victory of emancipation at the hands of law enforcement and their accomplices, see Haley (2016).

5. In the introduction to *African American Women and the Vote: 1837–1965*, Ann D. Gordon opens the collection of essays that make up the proceedings of the 1991 conference at the University of Massachusetts Amherst with a tribute to the 1,603 African American women who "released a statement of conscience in November 1991, protesting the manipulation of Black History and 'malicious defamation' of women that marked the confirmation hearings of Judge Clarence Thomas to the bench of the United States Supreme Court." Their statement appeared in the *New York Times*, November 17, 1991, and was titled "African American Women in Defense of Themselves" (2–8).

6. It is important to note that on the first day of the conference, aside from the keynote speaker, myself, and a SUNY New Paltz lecturer, we were the only clearly identifiable black women in the room. After giving this talk as part of the "Limits of Suffrage" panel the next day, one of the white women who had seen the panel came up to me personally during a break to

appreciate me for being one of two presenters that day who used the word "intersectionality" to speak to the work of women's struggles for the vote.

7. I borrow this instructive turn of phrase from the Latina Feminist Collective's "Telling to Live: A Feminist of Color Theory," the introduction of *Telling to Live: Latina Feminist Testimonios* which states, "From our different personal, political, ethnic, and academic trajectories, we arrived at the importance of *testimonio* as a crucial means of bearing witness and inscribing into history those lived realities that would otherwise succumb to the alchemy of erasure" (Acevedo 2001, 4). In class discussion at Vassar College (during spring 2018), my students grappled with the meaning of this phrase and collectively divined its meaning as indicative of both the magical thinking that falsifies and invalidates the science that informs feminist of color politics and the persistent power preserved in the upholding of its erasure of colonial violence as a precious product of the magical thinking of empire, conquest, and patriarchy.

8. In addition, like moral reformers, neither suffragists nor free lovers paid attention to the sexual vulnerability of African American women, nor did they take note of the escalating racial violence they faced. Not unlike the fatal consequences of alleged rape accusations against black men, black women's innocence was never presumed. Rather, suffragists and anarchists sought to empower white women to resist rape by expanding their political and thereby their sexual rights at the expense of black liberation—for more, see Freedman (2013).

Works Cited

Acevedo, Luz A. 2001. *Telling to Live: Latina Feminist Testimonios*. Durham, NC: Duke University Press.

Camp, Stephanie 2004. *Closer to Freedom: Enslaved Women and Everyday Resistance in the Plantation South*. Chapel Hill: University of North Carolina Press.

Campbell, Grace P. 1925. "Tragedy of the Colored Girl in Court." https://search. alexanderstreet.com/view/work/bibliographic_entity%7Cbibliographic_ details%7C2737169.

Davis, Angela Y. 1972. "Reflections on the Black Woman's Role in the Community of Slaves." *Massachusetts Review* 13, no. 1/2 (Winter–Spring): 81–100.

Davis, Angela Y. 2011. *Women, Race & Class*. New York: Vintage.

Davis, Angela Y. 2013. "Feminism and Abolition: Theories and Practices for the Twenty-First Century." Public Lecture, University of Chicago, May 2013.

Freedman, Estelle B. 2013. *Redefining Rape: Sexual Violence in the Era of Suffrage and Segregation*. Cambridge, MA: Harvard University Press.

Gilmore, Ruth W. 2007. *Golden Gulag: Prisons, Surplus, Crisis, and Opposition in Globalizing California*. Berkeley: University of California Press.

Goodier, Susan. 2017. "Historian's Corner: Seeking and Seeing Black Women: Hester C. Jeffrey and Woman Suffrage Activism." *New York History* 98, no. 3–4 (Fall/Winter): 475–88.

Gordon, Ann D., and Bettye Collier-Thomas. 1997. *African American Women and the Vote, 1837–1965*. Amherst: University of Massachusetts Press.

Haley, Sarah. 2016. *No Mercy Here: Gender, Punishment, and the Making of Jim Crow Modernity*. Chapel Hill: University of North Carolina Press.

Jacobs, Harriet A., Lydia Maria Child, and Jean Fagan Yellin. 1987. *Incidents in the Life of a Slave Girl: Written by Herself*. Cambridge, MA: Harvard University Press.

Jones, Beverly W. 1982. "Mary Church Terrell and the National Association of Colored Women, 1896 to 1901." *Journal of Negro History* 67, no. 1 (Spring): 20–33.

Lorde, Audre. 2015. *Sister Outsider: Essays and Speeches*. Berkeley, CA: Crossing Press.

National Association of Colored Women's Clubs. 1978. *A History of the Club Movement among the Colored Women of the United States of America: As Contained in the Minutes of the Conventions, Held in Boston, July 29, 30, 31, 1895, and of the National Federation of Afro-American Women, Held in Washington, D.C., July 20, 21, 22, 1896*. Washington, DC: The Association.

Smith, Barbara. 1979. "Racism and Women's Studies." *Frontiers: A Journal of Women Studies* 5, no. 1 (Spring): 48–49.

Stanton, Elizabeth Cady Susan B. Anthony, Matilda J. Gage, and Ida H. Harper. 1985. *History of Woman Suffrage*. Salem, NH: Ayer.

Stewart, Maria W. 2010. "An Address Delivered Before the African-American Female Intelligence Society of America." In *Women's Work: An Anthology of African-American Women's Historical Writings from Antebellum America to the Harlem Renaissance*, edited by Laurie F. Maffly-Kipp and Kathryn Lofton. New York: Oxford University Press.

Terborg-Penn, Rosalyn. 1999. *African American Women in the Struggle for the Vote, 1850–1920*. Bloomington: Indiana University Press.

Chapter 9

Which Way Forward?

Freedom Organizing in the Twenty-First Century

BARBARA SMITH[1]

Barbara Smith, noted activist, writer, and former Albany Common Council member, provided the conference's keynote address. In her remarks, Smith discussed contemporary politics, at the state and national levels, through the lens of her decades of experience as an organizer in myriad rights movements. In so doing, Smith asks activists, academics, and all invested participants to reflect on the weaknesses of movements, historically and at present, that are not truly intersectional in their interpretations and approaches.

Smith's analysis elucidates the historic tension in women's activism for gender justice because it often occurred at the expense of racial justice. As many of the chapters in this volume make clear, women's political movements—both to gain the vote and in its after-math—have at times ignored white supremacy or made peace with it for political expediency. Smith's speech instructs that acknowledging this past—learning from it and proceeding with intentionality and integrity in the face of all systems of oppression—provides the only path for successful feminist political activism. As Smith argues, "The way forward is to be engaged in freedom organizing that does not merely address the symptoms of oppression, but that also comprehends and challenges the reasons for it." Such a reckoning will be neither easy nor always comfortable, yet it is possible and imperative: "It takes courage and experience to interrupt bigotry . . . but . . . it is a

145

part of our responsibility as humans to learn how to do it." The talk concluded with five recommendations for how activists might do so in the future.

‿

In 1979, in Lawrence, Kansas, I delivered a closing address at the first annual conference of the National Women's Studies Association. The title of my speech was "Racism and Women's Studies." At the time, the need to approach women's studies from an antiracist and inclusive perspective was not something that most of the practitioners in this just-beginning field even considered. White feminists also seldom took race into account in the wider women's movement. I explained in my speech that the reason racism is a feminist issue is because of the inherent meaning of feminism. I then offered the following definition: "Feminism is the political theory and practice that struggles to free all women: women of color, working-class women, poor women, disabled women, Jewish women, lesbians, old women—as well as white, economically privileged heterosexual women. Anything less than this vision of total freedom is not feminism, but merely female self-aggrandizement" (Smith 1998, 96). Since then, some have embraced the multiracial, multi-issued politics that this definition embodies. The concept of intersectionality that legal scholar Kimberlé Crenshaw introduced in the late 1980s has also helped people to understand that it is critical to take into account interlocking identities and oppressions in order to make meaningful social and political change.

When we look at the history of the struggle for woman suffrage, we see that racism and class oppression undermined the organizing and weakened the movement. Solidarity across racial lines would have been quite remarkable at a time when social segregation and assumptions of Black inferiority were universally acceptable. Despite their mistreatment by white women, Black women nevertheless fought for the vote.

In the twenty-first century, the specific impact of race, ethnicity, gender, gender expression, sexuality, class, religion, and immigration status continues to create divisions within feminism. When women called for a march on Washington following the 2016 presidential election, there was immediate concern about which women. Would this march and its visible leadership reflect the experiences and issues of the multiplicity of women in this nation and around the globe, or would it fall back on a racially and economically exclusive, not to mention very tired, version of feminism? Fortunately, those who originated the call for the march quickly understood the need to be as inclusive as possible, and a diverse group of women of color became lead organizers. By deciding to be inclusive, the march organizers were also making a decision to be accountable, to at least raise questions about how privilege can affect one's understanding of what women's issues actually are.

When the Women's March released their "Guiding Vision and Definition of Principles," their platform showed a clear commitment to intersectional feminism. Reading it, I recalled the definition of feminism that I had offered decades before and felt gratified that the politics that feminists of color have struggled for so long to become integrated into the broader women's movement were finally being acknowledged and having real impact upon women's organizing in the most visible of contexts. I believe a critical factor in the historic success of the Women's Marches all over the nation and the globe was their more expansive vision of feminism.

Here is an excerpt from the march's platform:

** We believe that Women's Rights are Human Rights and Human Rights are Women's Rights. This is the basic and original tenet from which all our values stem.

** We believe Gender Justice is Racial Justice is Economic Justice. We must create a society in which women—in particular Black women, Native women, poor women, immigrant women, Muslim women, and queer and trans women—are free and able to care for and nurture their families, however they are formed, in safe and healthy environments free from structural impediments. (Women's March on Washington 2017, 2)[2]

The genuinely progressive political theory and practice that feminists of color have built over the decades is just what is needed in these perilous times.

The triumph of January 21 seems like it happened years ago. Our communities are now under constant assault from this administration:

immigrants; refugees; working people; women; the LGBTQ community, especially people who are transgender; people struggling in poverty; people of color; people with disabilities, just to name a few. But we also are seeing remarkable resistance and even some victories. As incredible as the women's marches were, to me, the nationwide response to the predator in chief's first Muslim ban was in some ways even more amazing because these actions were not the result of weeks or even days of planning. As soon as the executive order attacking Muslims was issued, people flocked to airports all over the country to protest. The images of attorneys with laptops sitting on the floors of airports working hour after hour to restore human rights and to free people from a government gone berserk, while huge, vibrant crowds protested the injustice in a way that could not be ignored (some wearing pink hats), was unforgettable. I loved the airport protests since it was clear that people knew what to do because they had functioning moral compasses and also because they had prior experience of organizing. Would people have gone to the airports in such numbers if they had not seen the example of the protests that started the day after the election and the massive Women's Marches just the week before?[3]

As a lifelong activist, I have rarely been so busy, but that is what these times require. My title asks the question "Which Way Forward?" and includes the answer. The way forward is to be engaged in freedom organizing that does not merely address the symptoms of oppression but also comprehends and challenges the reasons for it. In early February, I was invited to participate in the national planning group for the International Women's Strike U.S., which took place worldwide on March 8. This was a wonderful opportunity for people to mobilize around issues that affect women, understood with an explicitly anticapitalist, antiracist, and anti-imperialist perspective. The Women's Strike U.S. is continuing to organize around an intersectional political agenda and is now working in coalition with other groups on May Day actions focused upon immigrant rights.[4]

Because our situation is so dire, I believe that the passion for justice is rising to match it. It is in times like these that human beings often exceed what they would have previously thought possible. It is not that I want to see people suffer. I have spent many sleepless nights since November 8 [2016], thinking about the horrors that those without access to power and privilege are so heartlessly being forced to endure. But we have to find hope and inspiration where we can. We need to study what our ancestors did under the worst of circumstances and then see what we can do ourselves. There is always something we can do.

A few weeks ago, I did a presentation for the Interfaith Alliance in the Capital District. A young white gay man described an encounter with a store clerk when he accompanied a friend of his who is a lesbian of color to the grocery store. His friend was using an EBT card. When the clerk saw her method of payment, she began to berate and insult her. He did not know what to do. He didn't say anything at the time and then asked me what he could have done. I suggested that he could have said, "It's not necessary for you to speak to my friend like that." Afterward it occurred to me he could also have said, "The way you are talking to my friend makes me very uncomfortable." Unlike my first suggestion, the second focused more upon how he felt about what was going on instead of only making a judgment about the clerk's behavior. It also occurred to me that he could have simply asked, "Why are you talking that way?" It takes courage and experience to interrupt bigotry, but I think it is a part of our responsibility as humans to learn how to do it.

Unfortunately, in the next few years we are going to get a lot of practice. When I was invited to speak last fall, I had no idea that I would be doing so in the midst of what many consider a crisis for our nation. While preparing my remarks, I thought about how much time I should devote to "45" and the white patriarchs he has picked to scourge the country. I thought about how this speech might have been different based upon a different outcome of the presidential election. I realized, however, that the basic message about the need for us continually to work for freedom and justice is not fundamentally altered by what we now face. White supremacy, misogyny, poverty, homophobia, transphobia, mass incarceration, militarism, and environmental devastation would be in place whoever occupied the White House. With the current situation, we will have even more work to do; many more of us need to commit to the struggle, and we also need to be even smarter and more strategic in our organizing.

Although the outcome of November's election [2016] is the result of a number of factors, I think it is particularly important to consider that this presidency has been brought to us by the United States' refusal to confront white supremacy and to eradicate it. I want to clarify what I mean by white supremacy. What the civil rights movement and subsequent antiracist organizing addressed, and did so with some success, was segregation and discrimination: in schools, in voting, in employment, in public accommodations, and more. Legal barriers to equality have fallen and many social barriers among the races have diminished, but at the end of the day the institution of white supremacy is still intact. It can be difficult for us to understand the distinction between discrimination and institutionalized oppression since this topic is seldom explored. Usually when people speak about racism, they are referring to prejudice in the context of interpersonal relations. It is extremely important to change prejudiced attitudes and actions that disparage, hurt, and endanger people of color, but this alone does not get to the overarching system of entrenched inequality. As I mentioned, there have been many interventions to topple the separate and unequal, second-class citizenship of the Jim Crow era, yet magically, racial oppression still remains.

Here are a few examples of how white supremacy functions. Recent research demonstrates that Black people across the board are offered less effective pain management than white people when they seek medical care. Some of those surveyed were doctors who were still being trained at the beginning of their careers. Despite the fact that they came of age decades after Jim Crow, they nevertheless offer inadequate pain medication to Black patients much as one would expect older physicians to do. This reflects an institutional pattern of oppression driven by stereotypes and attitudes about Black bodies which the physicians might not even know they hold (Hoffman et al. 2016, 4296–4301).

Another example is the way in which banks treat Black and Latino customers, especially those applying for loans. During the subprime mortgage crisis, a huge percentage of those who lost their homes were people of color because they had been disproportionately pushed into bad loans by financial institutions. Outrageously, this group included people of color who were actually qualified for much better loan options. Although the mortgage crisis is officially over, this practice still continues. The fact that Black households' median wealth in 2013 was $11,000 while white households had $141,900, thirteen times as much, is not because Black people do not work as hard or do not manage their finances well. The wealth gap reflects the economic consequences of white supremacy and is one of the starkest and most definitive examples of institutionalized racism (Kochhar and Fry 2014).

Mass incarceration is perhaps the most blatant example of the persistence of white supremacy. Michelle Alexander's (2010) pivotal work *The New Jim Crow* is a damning indictment of our unjust criminal justice system. A recent series of articles in the *New York Times* documents how Black prisoners are consistently singled out for harsher disciplinary treatment, including solitary confinement and brutal physical attacks, by predominantly white guards in upstate prisons (Schwirtz, Winerip, and Gebeloff 2016).

One way to determine if institutional racism is occurring is to look at widespread, research-vetted statistical trends. All of these examples have that in common.

Institutionalized racism would be a threat whoever won the presidency. It is simply a more extreme threat now because the president's bigoted rhetoric was an important factor in the election and he and his administration have a record of promoting all forms of bigotry, including racism, anti-Semitism, xenophobia, misogyny, homophobia, and transphobia.

I want to conclude by discussing principles and practices that will help us to survive, endure, and ultimately win.

First of all, you cannot go it alone. The only way to have an impact and to make meaningful political, economic, and social change is to work with others, to find those who share your vision and work together as a community. I believe in grassroots organizing and also in the brilliance of collective intelligence. None of us has all the answers on our own, but when we share our perspectives and insight, we can come up with remarkable strategies and solutions.

Second, it is critical that those who are the most targeted by oppression get to define the agenda and lead the organizing to challenge that injustice. One of the reasons that the Southern civil rights movement was so effective, for example with the Montgomery bus boycott, was that Black people bravely stood up against white supremacy on their own behalf. The boycott lasted 381 days. People walked and organized their own alternative transportation for more than a year. Voter registration campaigns in the rural South were driven by the indigenous leadership of those whose rights had been nullified for centuries. Fannie Lou Hamer and the Mississippi Freedom

Democratic Party come immediately to mind. Their organizing led to the Voting Rights Act of 1965.

Third, we cannot engage in single-issue struggles. Even if we are focused upon a particular cause, we need to stay alert and take every opportunity to work in coalition and to practice genuine solidarity.

Fourth, we need to find joy in the struggle. Working for justice can fill our souls if we feel respected and seen and actually like the people with whom we work. We can also stay in it for the long haul by taking care of ourselves and taking time to do whatever you consider fun. There is a young Black woman organizer in Albany who is very active in Black Lives Matter and who is a full-time organizer focused upon educational justice. I was delighted to find out that she loves the outdoors, is an experienced camper, and connects with nature every chance she gets. Early in her activist life she has found a great way to keep her balance and to keep her spirit whole. Activism should not make you miserable. If it does, you should look for other contexts in which to do your activism.

Finally, we need to recognize that we are engaged in a long struggle. It began before we got here and will continue after we are gone. We can take courage and inspiration from our ancestors. We can feel encouraged by some wins. Five million people at the Women's Marches is a win. More than fifty actions all over the country for the International Women's Strike on March 8, 2017 is also a win. The fact that both of the Muslim bans have been blocked by the courts is a big win. The fact that the attempt to repeal and replace the Affordable Care Act (Obamacare) spectacularly failed is a win. This last win occurred in no small part because of the thousands of ordinary people who spoke out at town hall meetings all over the country and let their legislators know that they did not want to lose their access to affordable health care.

In more than fifty years of organizing, I have found no magic solutions to eradicating oppression, except to be involved in struggle. We will not be able to fix everything at once, but every single day each of us can absolutely do our part to work for justice.

Notes

1. The editors thank Denise Oliver-Velez for her essential role in inviting Barbara Smith to give the conference's keynote address and delivering the opening remarks for Smith's speech.

2. As the Women's March developed, its organizers have prioritized more mainstream electoral solutions. The theme of the 2018 Women's March in Las Vegas was "Power to the Polls."

3. A person familiar with the breadth of immigrant rights organizing pointed out to me that although the demonstrations seemed spontaneous, they could not have occurred if there had not been a well-organized movement already in place. Undoubtedly, immigrant rights and Muslim organizations had discussed strategies for how to respond if the ban was issued.

4. For more, see WomenStrikeUS.org.

Works Cited

Alexander, Michelle. 2010. *The New Jim Crow: Mass Incarceration in the Age of Colorblindness*. New York: New Press.

Hoffman, Kelly M., Sophie Trawalter, Jordan R. Axt, and M. Norman Oliver. 2016. "Racial Bias in Pain Assessment and Treatment Recommendations, and False Beliefs about Biological Differences between Blacks and Whites." *Proceedings of the National Academy of Sciences* 113, no. 16 (April): 4296–301.

Kochhar, Rakesh, and Richard Fry. 2014. "Wealth Inequality Has Widened along Racial, Ethnic Lines Since End of Great Recession. Pew Research Center. December 12, 2014. http://www.pewresearch.org/fact tank/2014/12/12/racial-wealth-gaps-great-recession/.

Schwirtz, Michael, Michael Winerip, and Robert Gebeloff. 2016. "The Scourge of Racial Bias in New York State's Prisons." *New York Times*, December 3, 2016. https://www.nytimes.com/2016/12/03/nyregion/new-york-state-prisons-inmates-racial-bias.html.

Smith, Barbara. 1998. *The Truth That Never Hurts: Writings on Race Gender and Freedom*. New Brunswick, NJ: Rutgers University Press.

Women's March on Washington. 2017. "Guiding Vision and Definition of Principles." Last modified 2019. https://womensmarch.com/mission-and-principles.

APPENDIX

Women in Politics

Past, Present, and Future

**A Conference Commemorating the Centennial
of Women's Suffrage in New York State**

Friday, April 21, 2017 FDR Library and Museum

CONFERENCE SCHEDULE

2:00 p.m.   *Arrival & Registration*
            Opportunity to explore the museum

4:00 p.m.   *Greetings & Theme Setting, Milstein Auditorium*
            Paul Sparrow, Director, FDR Presidential Library and
                Museum
            Dr. Susan Lewis, Conference Chair, Department of
                History, SUNY New Paltz

4:30 p.m.   Senator Kirsten Gillibrand

5:00 p.m.   *Women in Politics: Women @ Work 2017 NYS Views on
            Women (VOW) Poll*
            Dr. Eve Waltermaurer, Director of Research &
                Evaluation, The Benjamin Center, SUNY New
                Paltz

5:15 p.m.   *Stories of Success: Women Winning & Leading*
             Moderator: *Capital Tonight* Host Liz Benjamin
             Panelists:
                State Senator Marisol Alcantara (District 31)
                Rensselaer County Executive Kathleen Jimino
                Albany Mayor Kathy Sheehan
                Christine Quinn, Speaker of the New York City
                   Council (2006–2013)

6:00 p.m.   *Cocktail Reception & Toast, Lobby*
             Dr. Wylecia Wiggs Harris, Chief Executive Officer,
               League of Women Voters of the US
             Dare Thompson, President, League of Women Voters
               of NYS

7:00 p.m.   *Dinner, Multipurpose Room*

8:00 p.m.   *Keynote Address*
             "Eleanor Roosevelt, the Politician, and Woman
               Suffrage: A Conversation with Allida Black and
               Anne Lewis"

SATURDAY, APRIL 22, 2017 SUNY NEW PALTZ LECTURE CENTER

8:00 a.m.   *Check-in & Continental Breakfast, South Lobby*

8:30 a.m.   *Greetings & Theme Setting, LC 100*
             President Donald Christian New York Lieutenant
               Governor Kathy Hochul
             Kathleen Dowley, PhD, Associate Professor of Political
               Science & International Relations; Coordinator,
               Women's Gender & Sexuality Studies Program

9:00 a.m.   *Concurrent Sessions*

LC 102   "1917: How Did Women Win the Vote in New York
               State?"
             Moderator: Susan Lewis, PhD, Associate Professor of
               History, SUNY New Paltz Panelists:
             Susan Goodier, PhD, Lecturer in History, SUNY Oneonta

Karen Pastorello, PhD, Professor of History, Tompkins
Cortland Community College

Lauren Santangelo, PhD, Author, *The "Feminized" City:
New York and Suffrage, 1870–1917*

LC 104   "Women in Government Today"
Moderator: Ş. İlgü Özler, PhD, Associate Professor
of Political Science & Director, SUNY Global
Engagement Program Panelists:
kt Tobin, PhD, Associate Director, The Benjamin
Center
Kira Sanbonmatsu, PhD, Professor of Political
Science & Senior Scholar, Center for American
Women and Politics, Rutgers University
Pamela Paxton, PhD, Professor of Sociology &
Public Affairs, University of Texas at Austin

10:15 a.m. *Coffee Break, South Lobby*

10:30 a.m. *Concurrent Sessions*

LC 102   "After the Vote: Women in Social and Political
Movements"
Moderator: Meg Devlin O'Sullivan, PhD, Assistant
Professor of History and Women's, Gender &
Sexuality Studies, SUNY New Paltz Panelists:
Joanna L. Grossman, Professor of Law, SMU
Dedman School of Law
Julie A. Gallagher, PhD, Assistant Professor of History
and Women's Studies, Penn State University
Jennifer Guglielmo, PhD, Professor of History,
Smith College

LC 104   "The Limits of Suffrage in a Liberal Democracy"
Moderator: Kathleen Dowley, PhD, SUNY New Paltz
Panelists:
Jasmine Syedullah, PhD, Visiting Assistant Professor
of Critical Race & Ethnic Studies, Vassar College
Amy Baehr, PhD, Associate Professor of Philosophy,
Hofstra University

Kate Manne, PhD, Assistant Professor of Philosophy, Cornell University

11:45 p.m.   *Lunch, South Lobby*

12:30 p.m.   *Keynote Address, LC 100*
"Which Way Forward? Freedom Organizing in the Twenty-First Century"
Barbara Smith, Black Feminist Author & Activist

1:15 p.m.   *Concurrent Sessions*

LC 102   "Women in New York State: The Unfinished Agenda"
Moderator: Jessica Pabón, PhD, Assistant Professor of Women's, Gender, & Sexuality Studies, SUNY New Paltz
Panelists:
   Kelly Baden, Director of State Advocacy, Center for Reproductive Rights
   Katherine Cross, PhD Student in Sociology, CUNY Graduate Center
   Irene Jor, New York Organizer, National Domestic Workers Alliance
   Callie Jayne, Community Organizer, Citizen Action of New York

LC 104   *K–12 Teacher Workshop*
Incorporating Women's Political History into K–12 Curriculum Sponsored by Mohonk Mountain House

CONTRIBUTORS

Amy R. Baehr is associate professor of philosophy at Hofstra University, where she teaches legal and political philosophy and women's studies. Her scholarship explores the possibility of a feminist liberal political philosophy. She serves on the executive committee of the New York Society for Women in Philosophy and on the American Philosophical Association's Committee on the Status of Women. Recent papers include "A Capacious Account of Liberal Feminism" (forthcoming in *Feminist Philosophy Quarterly*), "Feminist Receptions of the Original Position" in *The Original Position* (2015), and "Feminism, Perfectionism, and Public Reason" (*Law and Philosophy*, 2008). She is editor of *Varieties of Feminist Liberalism* and author of the *Stanford Encyclopedia of Philosophy* entry on liberal feminism.

Gabrielle Baron-Hill has spent a lifetime lifting people up, whether through a heartfelt conversation on the street or through her loving and wise counsel, collaborating with diverse groups on an array of community initiatives. A proud Newburgh native, Gabrielle overcame adversity and worked her way through the service industry to become a mentor at the Center for Hope, where she collaborated with young people on the issue of sexual assault. More recently, Gabrielle has led the Newburgh (founding) chapter of the Restorative Center as program director, facilitating the Circles program that draws locals and newcomers alike to learn from one another and gather collective wisdom on challenging issues that affect all residents. She also serves as executive director assistant at Northwestern Human Services, supporting the social service staff and lending support to families who are at risk. She is also dedicated to unearthing the rich, untold black history in

Newburgh, knowing that when people understand their past from a view of contribution, they have a different perspective of the present and future. Gabrielle is honored to be recognized by MVP Health as a Black Pioneer of Newburgh, and she received recognition as Parent of the Month, July 2015, in the *Hudson Valley Parent* magazine.

Kathleen M. Dowley is associate professor and chair of the Department of Political Science and International Relations at the State University of New York at New Paltz. She received her PhD in political science from Michigan State University and her MA in Russian and East European studies from the University of Michigan. Her research and teaching focus on comparative European politics, ethnic politics, and women and politics. She conducts cross-national research on the role of political culture and public opinion in the governance of multiethnic states, and her articles have been published in a variety of journals, including *Comparative Political Studies, Communist and Post-Communist Studies*, and the *International Journal of Public Opinion Research*.

Julie A. Gallagher is associate professor of history and women's studies at Penn State Brandywine. She received her PhD in history from the University of Massachusetts Amherst; an MA in education from the University of Michigan; a BA in economics from Fordham University; and a certificate in international relations at Columbia University's School of International and Public Affairs (SIPA). Her book *Black Women and Politics in New York City* (2014) traces the evolution of African American women as political actors in various roles—as activists, voters, appointees, and elected officials—across seven decades. Professor Gallagher's current research examines how, why, and to what effect members of civil society who engage in activism, especially in periods of state upheaval, tap into the discursive, policy, and normative resources of international bodies, especially the United Nations, to challenge oppressive practices within their homelands.

Susan Goodier studies US women's activism, particularly woman suffrage activism, from 1840 to 1920. She did her graduate work at SUNY at Albany, earning a master's degree in gender history and a doctorate in public policy history, with subfields in international gender and culture and black women's studies. She then completed a second master's degree in women's studies. At the State University of

New York at Oneonta, she teaches courses in women's history, New York State history, the Civil War and Reconstruction, and Progressive Era history. Dr. Goodier is an Organization of American Historians distinguished lecturer and the coordinator for the Upstate New York Women's History Organization (UNYWHO). She is also the book review editor for the journal *New York History*. The University of Illinois published her first book, *No Votes for Women: The New York State Anti-Suffrage Movement*, in 2013. Her second book, *Women Will Vote: Winning Suffrage in New York State*, coauthored with Karen Pastorello, was published by Cornell University Press in 2017, helping to mark the centennial of women voting in New York State.

Joanna L. Grossman is the inaugural Ellen K. Solender Endowed Chair in Women and the Law at Southern Methodist University Dedman School of Law. After graduating with distinction from Stanford Law School, Professor Grossman began her career as a clerk for Ninth Circuit Judge William A. Norris. She also worked as staff counsel at the National Women's Law Center in Washington, DC, as a recipient of the Women's Law and Public Policy Fellowship. Professor Grossman writes extensively on sex discrimination and workplace equality, with a particular focus on issues such as sexual harassment and pregnancy discrimination. Her most recent book, *Nine to Five: How Gender, Sex, and Sexuality Continue to Define the American Workplace* (2016), provides a lively and accessible discussion of contemporary cases and events that show gender continues to define the work experience in both predictable and surprising ways.

Susan Ingalls Lewis is professor emerita, formerly deputy chair and graduate advisor in the Department of History at the State University of New York at New Paltz, as well as an affiliate faculty member in the Women's, Gender, and Sexuality Studies Program. Dr. Lewis received her BA from Wellesley College and her PhD from Binghamton University. She teaches courses on American history, American women's history, and New York State history. Her monograph *Unexceptional Women: Female Proprietors in Mid-Nineteenth-Century Albany, New York, 1830–1885* (2009) won the Hagley Prize in Business History for the best book published in the field (2011). Professor Lewis has also been named Liberal Arts & Sciences Teacher of the Year (2007–2008), has won the Liberal Arts & Sciences Excellence in Scholarship Award

(2011), and was honored with a SUNY Chancellor's Award for Excellence in Teaching (2017). Dr. Lewis is a fellow of the New York Academy of History and author of the blog *New York Rediscovered*.

Meg Devlin O'Sullivan is associate professor of history and women's, gender, and sexuality studies at the State University of New York at New Paltz. She earned her BA in history and women's studies at the University of Wisconsin-Madison and PhD in history at the University of North Carolina at Chapel Hill. She teaches and publishes in the areas of Native American history, US women's history, and feminist pedagogy. Her most recent work has appeared in *Women's History Review*; *Journal of Family History*; *Atlantis: Critical Studies in Gender, Culture & Social Justice*; *The Native South: New Histories and Enduring Legacies* (2017); and *Teaching History: A Journal of Methods*.

Karen Pastorello formerly chaired the Women and Gender Studies Program at Tompkins Cortland Community College. She is author, most recently, of *Women Will Vote: Winning Suffrage in New York State* (2017), with Susan Goodier. She has published several articles and two other books: *A Power Among Them: Bessie Abramowitz Hillman and the Making of the Amalgamated Clothing Workers of America* (2008) and *The Progressives: Activism and Reform in American Society, 1893–1917* (2014). She earned a PhD in modern American history from Binghamton University, an MA in American labor history from Arizona State University, and a BA in history and education from St. John Fisher College. Dr. Pastorello taught at Tompkins Cortland Community College for thirty years. She taught the American history survey courses as well as Nineteenth Century Labor History, US Women's History, and Women and Work. Her interests include Progressive Era labor history and labor feminism.

Kira Sanbonmatsu is professor of political science at Rutgers University and senior scholar at the Center for American Women and Politics (CAWP) at the Eagleton Institute of Politics. Her research interests include gender, race/ethnicity, parties, public opinion, and state politics. Her most recent book (with Susan J. Carroll) is *More Women Can Run: Gender and Pathways to the State Legislatures* (2013). She is the coauthor (with Susan J. Carroll and Debbie Walsh) of the CAWP report *Poised to Run: Women's Pathways to the State Legislatures* (2009).

She is also the author of *Where Women Run: Gender and Party in the American States* (2006) and *Democrats, Republicans, and the Politics of Women's Place* (2002). Her articles have appeared in such journals as the *American Journal of Political Science, Politics & Gender* and *Party Politics*. She coedits the CAWP Series in Gender and American Politics at the University of Michigan Press with Susan J. Carroll. Sanbonmatsu received her BA from the University of Massachusetts Amherst and her PhD from Harvard University.

Barbara Smith is an author, activist, and independent scholar who has played a groundbreaking role in opening up a national cultural and political dialogue about the intersections of race, class, sexuality, and gender. She has been politically active in many movements for social justice since the 1960s. She was cofounder and, until 1995, publisher of Kitchen Table: Women of Color Press, the first national publisher in the United States for women of color. She served two terms as a member of the Albany Common Council and is currently the special community projects coordinator for the City of Albany, helping to implement the Equity Agenda. She is a regular panelist on WAMC Northeast Public Radio's *The Roundtable.*

Jasmine Syedullah is an abolitionist, academic, and coauthor of *Radical Dharma: Talking Race, Love, and Liberation* (2016). She is currently visiting assistant professor of critical race and ethnic studies at Vassar College. Syedullah holds a PhD in politics, with a designated emphasis in feminist studies and history of consciousness, from the University of California, Santa Cruz, and a BA from Brown University in religious studies, with a focus in Buddhist philosophy. Her current book (in progress), *No Selves to Defend: Living in the Loopholes of Legal Recognition*, rethinks the protocols of modern domesticity, legality, freedom, and sovereignty through black fugitive practices of abolition that shift the sexual politics of patriarchal institutions from the margins of abolitionist activism to the center of its critique of captivity.

Kathleen (kt) Tobin, director of the Benjamin Center at the State University of New York at New Paltz, is responsible for designing, managing, and producing projects focused on regional issues and concerns. Tobin earned her undergraduate degree in sociology from the State University of New York at New Paltz, her MS in social research from Hunter College of the City University of New York, and her PhD in sociology from SUNY Albany. Tobin is also an affiliated lecturer in sociology, teaching Introduction to Sociology, Social Inequality, Research Methods, and Women in Politics. Tobin is also a former school board member and currently the deputy mayor of the Village of New Paltz.

Eve Walter is a senior research scientist at the Institute for Family Health. Dr. Walter's personal research agenda centers primarily on women's health and women's status in the United States. Her publications include fifteen academic papers related specifically to women's issues, including domestic violence, contraception, and breastfeeding. In addition, Dr. Walter directed and produced a documentary film about women's sexual exploration. She is the principal investigator responsible for the Women@Work View on Women (VOW) poll conducted in New York in 2016 to precede the centennial of women's suffrage in New York State and to be repeated nationally in 2020.

INDEX

Note: Italicized page numbers with a *t* indicate tables; those with *f* indicate figures.

Printed in the USA
CPSIA information can be obtained
at www.ICGtesting.com
LVHW040256291123
764972LV00008B/512